GERMAN

in 10 minutes a day®

by Kristine Kershul, M.A., University of California, Santa Barbara

Consultant: Susan Worthington

Bilingual Books, Inc.

1719 West Nickerson Street, Seattle, WA 98119
Tel: (206) 284-4211 • Fax: (206) 284-3660
www.10minutesaday.com

First printing, May 2002

Can you say this?

(vahs)   *(ist)*   *(dahs)*
Was ist das?
what   is   that

(dahs)   *(ein)*   *(ice)*
Das ist ein Eis.
                an   ice-cream cone

(vir)   *(murk-ten)*   *(ein)*   *(ice)*
Wir möchten ein Eis.
we   would like

If you can say this, you can learn to speak German. You will be able to easily order wine, lunch, theater tickets, pastry, or anything else you wish. With your best German accent you simply ask „**Was ist das?**" *(vahs) (ist) (dahs)* and, upon learning what it is, you can order it with „**Wir möchten das**" *(vir) (murk-ten) (dahs)*. Sounds easy, doesn't it?

The purpose of this book is to give you an **immediate** speaking ability in German. German is spoken not only in Germany, but in Switzerland and Austria as well. Using the acclaimed "*10 minutes a day®*" methodology, you will acquire a large working vocabulary that will suit your needs, and you will acquire it almost automatically. To aid you, this book offers a unique and easy system of pronunciation above each word which walks you through learning German.

If you are planning a trip or moving to where German is spoken, you will be leaps ahead of everyone if you take just a few minutes a day to learn the easy key words that this book offers. Start with Step 1 and don't skip around. Each day work as far as you can comfortably go in those 10 minutes. Don't overdo it. Some days you might want to just review. If you forget a word, you can always look it up in the glossary. Spend your first 10 minutes studying the map on the previous page. And yes, have fun learning your new language.

As you work through the Steps, always use the special features which only this series offers. This book contains sticky labels and flash cards, free words, puzzles and quizzes. When you have completed the book, cut out the menu guide and take it along on your trip.

(dahs) *(ahl-fah-bate)*
Das Alphabet
the   alphabet

Above all new words is an easy pronunciation guide. Many German letters are pronounced just as they are in English, however, others are pronounced quite differently. Practice these sounds with the examples given which are mostly towns or areas in Europe which you might visit. Refer to this Step whenever you need help, but remember, spend no longer than 10 minutes a day.

German letter	English sound	Examples	Write it here
a	ah	**Alpen** *(ahl-pen)* Alps	_____
ä	ay	**Dänemark** *(day-nuh-mark)* Denmark	_____
au	ow / au	**Pass<u>au</u>** *(pahs-sau)*	_____
äu	oy	**Allg<u>äu</u>** *(ahl-goy)*	_____
b	b	**<u>B</u>asel** *(bah-zel)*	_____
***ch** *(varies)*	*(breathe hard)* H=hk / h / k	**Aa<u>ch</u>en** *(ah-Hen)*	_____
	sh	**Mün<u>ch</u>en** *(mewn-shen)*	_____
d	d	**<u>D</u>ortmund** *(dort-moont)*	_____
e *(varies)*	ay eh	**Br<u>e</u>men** *(bray-men)*	_____
e *(end of word)*	uh	**Elb<u>e</u>** *(el-buh)*	_____
ei	eye / ai / i / y	**<u>Ei</u>ger** *(eye-gair)*	_____
er	air	**B<u>er</u>lin** *(bair-leen)*	_____
eu	oy	**<u>Eu</u>ropa** *(oy-roh-pah)*	_____
f	f	**<u>F</u>rankfurt** *(frahnk-foort)*	_____
g *(as in good)*	g	**<u>G</u>enf** *(genf)* Geneva	_____
h	h	**<u>H</u>essen** *(hes-sen)*	_____
i	ih	**<u>I</u>nnsbruck** *(ins-brook)*	_____
ie	ee	**K<u>ie</u>l** *(keel)*	_____
j	y	**<u>J</u>ura** *(yoo-rah)*	_____

* This sound varies even among German speakers. The "H" is to help you remember to breathe hard while pronouncing an "hk" sound or even a gutteral "h." This will be your trickiest sound in German, but practice, practice, practice and you will master it.

German Letter	English Sound	Example	Write it here
k	k	**K**onstanz *(kohn-shtahnts)*	_____
l	l	**L**übeck *(lew-beck)*	_____
m	m	**M**annheim *(mahn-hime)*	_____
n	n	**N**euschwanstein *(noy-shvahn-shtine)* castle in southern Germany	_____
o	oh	**O**berammergau *(oh-bair-ah-mair-gau)*	_____
ö	ur / uhr	**Ö**sterreich *(uh-stair-rike)* Austria	_____
p	p	**P**otsdam *(pohts-dahm)*	_____
qu	kv	Mar**qu**artstein *(mar-kvart-shtine)*	_____
r	*(slightly rolled)* r	**R**ostock *(roh-shtohk)*	_____
s *(varies)*	s	Wie**s**baden *(vees-bah-den)*	_____
	z	Dre**s**den *(drayz-den)*	_____
sch	sh	**Sch**weiz *(shvites)*	_____
sp	shp	**Sp**eyer *(shpy-air)*	_____
st	sht	**St**uttgart *(shtoot-gart)*	_____
ß	ss	Me**ß**stetten *(mess-shtet-ten)*	_____
t	t	**T**irol *(tee-rohl)*	_____
th	t	**Th**un *(toon)*	_____
u	oo	**U**lm *(oolm)*	_____
ü	ew / ue	D**ü**sseldorf *(dew-sel-dorf)*	_____
v	f	**V**orarlberg *(for-arl-bairg)*	_____
w	v	**W**ien *(veen)* Vienna	_____
x	ks	Cu**x**haven *(kooks-hah-fen)*	_____
y	oo	S**y**lt *(soolt)*	_____
z	ts	Koblen**z** *(koh-blents)*	_____

Sometimes the phonetics may seem to contradict your pronunciation guide. Don't panic! The easiest and best possible phonetics have been chosen for each individual word. Pronounce the phonetics just as you see them. Don't over-analyze them. Speak with a German accent and, above all, enjoy yourself!

When you arrive in **Deutschland** *(doych-lahnt)* Germany or another German-speaking country, the very first thing you will need to do is ask questions — "Where **(wo)** *(voh)* where is the bus stop?" "**Wo** *(voh)* where can I exchange money?" "**Wo** *(voh)* is the lavatory?" "**Wo** is a restaurant?" "**Wo** do I catch a taxi?" "**Wo** is a good hotel?" "**Wo** is my luggage?" — and the list will go on and on for the entire length of your visit. In German, there are SEVEN KEY QUESTION WORDS to learn. For example, the seven key question words will help you find out exactly what you are ordering in a restaurant before you order it — and not after the surprise (or shock!) arrives. These seven key question words all begin with "**w**" which is pronounced like "v." Take a few minutes to study and practice saying the seven key question words listed below. Then cover the German with your hand and fill in each of the blanks with the matching German **Wort.** *(vort)* word

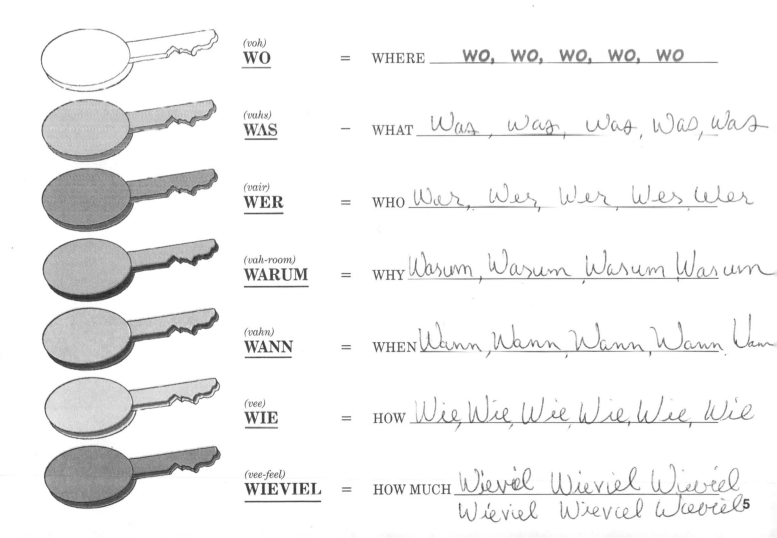

WO *(voh)*	=	WHERE	WO, WO, WO, WO, WO
WAS *(vuhs)*	–	WHAT	Was, Was, Was, Was, Was
WER *(vair)*	=	WHO	Wer, Wer, Wer, Wer, Wer
WARUM *(vah-room)*	=	WHY	Warum, Warum, Warum, Warum
WANN *(vahn)*	=	WHEN	Wann, Wann, Wann, Wann, Wann
WIE *(vee)*	=	HOW	Wie, Wie, Wie, Wie, Wie, Wie
WIEVIEL *(vee-feel)*	=	HOW MUCH	Wieviel Wieviel Wieviel Wieviel Wieviel Wieviel

5

Now test yourself to see if you really can keep these **Wörter** *(vur-tair)* straight in your mind. Draw lines words

between the German **und** *(oont)* English equivalents below. and

why   **wer** *(vair)*

what   **was** *(vahs)*

who   **wo** *(voh)*

how   **wieviel** *(vee-feel)*

where   **wann** *(vahn)*

when   **warum** *(vah-room)*

how much   **wie** *(vee)*

Examine the following questions containing these **Wörter** *(vur-tair)*. Practice the sentences out loud **und** *(oont)* and

then practice by copying the German in the blanks underneath each question.

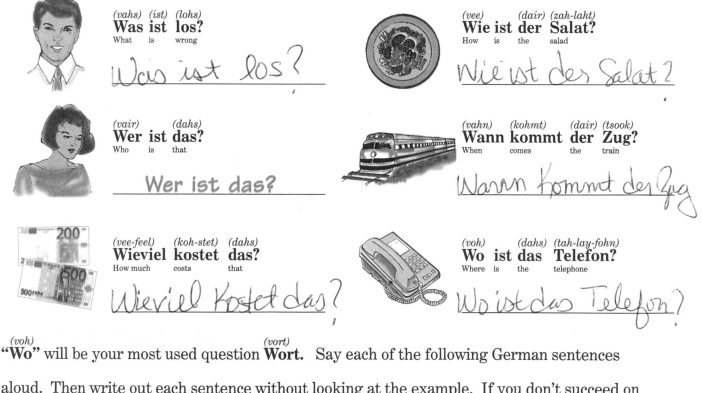

Was ist los? *(vahs) (ist) (lohs)*
What   is   wrong

Was ist los?

Wie ist der Salat? *(vee) (dair) (zah-laht)*
How   is   the   salad

Wie ist der Salat?

Wer ist das? *(vair) (dahs)*
Who   is   that

Wer ist das?

Wann kommt der Zug? *(vahn) (kohmt) (dair) (tsook)*
When   comes   the   train

Wann kommt der Zug

Wieviel kostet das? *(vee-feel) (koh-stet) (dahs)*
How much   costs   that

Wieviel kostet das?

Wo ist das Telefon? *(voh) (dahs) (tah-lay-fohn)*
Where   is   the   telephone

Wo ist das Telefon?

"**Wo**" *(voh)* will be your most used question **Wort.** *(vort)* Say each of the following German sentences

aloud. Then write out each sentence without looking at the example. If you don't succeed on

the first try, don't give up. Just practice each sentence until you are able to do it easily.

Remember "**ei**" is pronounced "eye" **und "ie"** is pronounced "ee." A "**g**" at the end of a word is

frequently pronounced like a "k."

(voh) (ist) (eye-nuh) (toy-let-tuh)
Wo ist eine Toilette?
Where   a   toilet

(voh) (ein) (tahk-see)
Wo ist ein Taxi?
Where is a taxi

(voh) (ein) (boos)
Wo ist ein Bus?
Where is bus

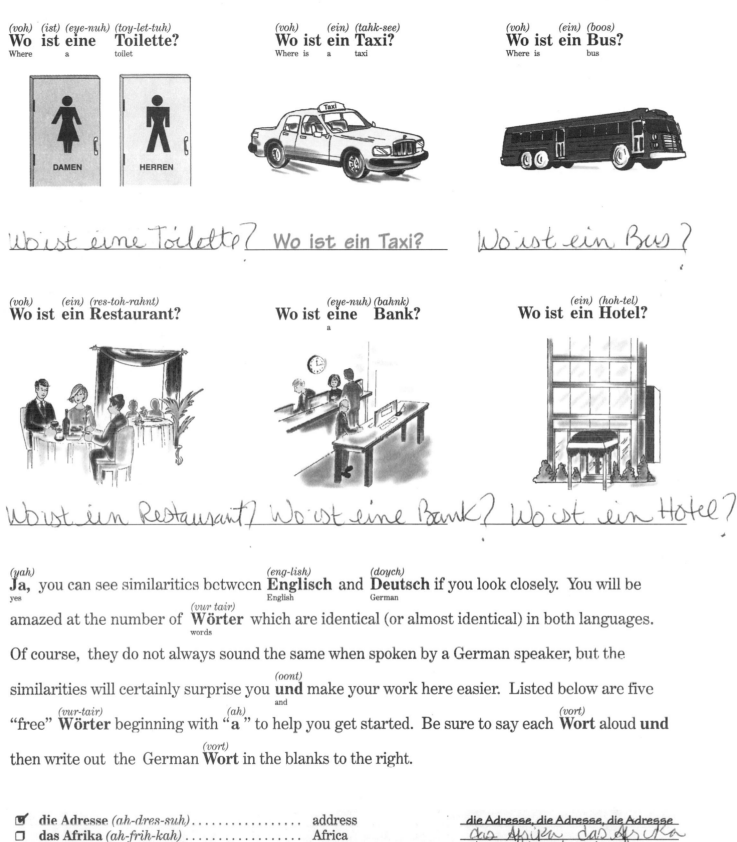

Wo ist eine Toilette?   Wo ist ein Taxi?   *Wo ist ein Bus?*

(voh) (ein) (res-toh-rahnt)
Wo ist ein Restaurant?

(eye-nuh) (bahnk)
Wo ist eine Bank?
a

(ein) (hoh-tel)
Wo ist ein Hotel?

Wo ist ein Restaurant?   Wo ist eine Bank?   Wo ist ein Hotel?

(yah)
Ja, you can see similarities between **Englisch** and **Deutsch** if you look closely. You will be
yes   English   German

(vur tair)
amazed at the number of **Wörter** which are identical (or almost identical) in both languages.
words

Of course, they do not always sound the same when spoken by a German speaker, but the

(oont)
similarities will certainly surprise you **und** make your work here easier. Listed below are five
and

(vur-tair)   (ah)   (vort)
"free" **Wörter** beginning with "**a**" to help you get started. Be sure to say each **Wort** aloud **und**

(vort)
then write out the German **Wort** in the blanks to the right.

☑	**die Adresse** (ah-dres-suh)	address	_die Adresse, die Adresse, die Adresse_
☐	**das Afrika** (ah-frih-kah)	Africa	*das Afrika das Afrika*
☐	**die Akademie** (ah-kah-deh-mee)	academy	**a** *die Akademie*
☐	**der Akt** (ahkt)	act (of a play)	*der Akt der Akt*
☐	**der Akzent** (ahk-tsent)	accent	*der Akzent der Akzent*

(vur-tair)
Free **Wörter** like these will appear at the bottom of the following pages in a yellow color band.

They are easy — enjoy them! Remember, in German, the letter "**ß**" is pronounced "ss."

7

Deutsch *(doych)* has multiple **Wörter** *(vur-tair)* for "the" and "a," but they are very easy.
German — words

| *(dair)* **der** the | *(dee)* **die** the | *(dahs)* **das** the | *(dehn)* **den** the | *(dehm)* **dem** the | *(des)* **des** the | | *(ein)* **ein** a | *(eye-nuh)* **eine** a | *(eye-nen)* **einen** a | *(eye-nair)* **einer** a | *(eye-nem)* **einem** a | *(eye-nes)* **eines** a |

der Mann *(mahn)*
the   man

die Frau *(frow)*
the   woman

das Kind *(kint)*
the   child

den Vater *(fah-tair)*
father

dem Fräulein *(froy-line)*
young woman

des Autos *(ow-tohs)*
car

ein Mann *(mahn)*
a   man

eine Frau *(frow)*
a   woman

ein Kind *(kint)*
a   child

einen Vater *(fah-tair)*
father

einem Fräulein *(froy-line)*
young woman

eines Autos *(ow-tohs)*

This might appear difficult at first, but only because it is different from **Englisch.** *(eng-lish)* Just remember you will be understood whether you say "**das Kind** *(kint)*" or "**die Kind**." Soon you will automatically select the right **Wort** without even thinking about it.

In Step 2 you were introduced to the Seven Key QuestionWords. These seven words are the basics, the most essential building blocks for learning German. Throughout this book you will come across keys asking you to fill in the missing question word. Use this opportunity not only to fill in the blank on that key, but to review all your question words. Play with the new sounds, speak slowly and have fun.

❑	**der Alkohol** *(ahl-koh-hohl)*	alcohol		*der Alkohol*
❑	**alle** *(ahl-luh)*	all		*alle*
❑	**das Amerika** *(ah-mair-ih-kah)*	America	**a**	*das America*
❑	**der Amerikaner** *(ah-mair-ih-kahn-air)*	American (male)		*des Americaner*
❑	**der Apfel** *(ahp-fel)*	apple		*der Apfel*

Before you proceed **mit** *(mit)* [with] this Step, situate yourself comfortably in your living room. Now look

around you. Can you name the things that you see in this **Zimmer** *(tsih-mair)* [room] in German? You can probably

guess **die Lampe** *(dee) (lahm-puh)* [the lamp] and maybe even **das Sofa** *(dahs) (zoh-fah)* [the sofa]. Let's learn the rest of them. After practicing

these **Wörter** *(vur-tair)* out loud, write them in the blanks below.

(dee) (lahm-puh)
die Lampe   *die Lampe*
lamp

(dahs) (zoh-fah)
das Sofa   *das Sofa*
sofa

(dair) (shtool)
der Stuhl   *der Stuhl*
chair

(tep-eeH)
der Teppich   *der Teppich*
carpet

(tish)
der Tisch   *der Tisch, der Tisch*
table

(dee) (tewr)
die Tür   *die Tür*
door

(oor)
die Uhr   *die Uhr*
clock

(dair) (for-hahng)
der Vorhang   *der Vorhang*
curtain

(tay-lay-fohn)
das Telefon   *das Telefon*
telephone

(fehn-stair)
das Fenster   *das Fenster*
window

(bilt)
das Bild   *das Bild*
picture

You will notice that the correct form of **der,** *(dair)* **die,** *(dee)* or **das** *(dahs)* is given **mit** [with] each noun. This tells you

whether the noun is masculine (**der**), feminine (**die**) or neuter (**das**). Now open your book to the

sticky labels on page 17 and later on page 35. Peel off the first 11 labels **und** *(oont)* [and] proceed around the

Zimmer *(tsih-mair)* [room] labeling these items in your home. This will help to increase your **deutsche** *(doy-chuh)* [German] **Wort** *(vort)* [word] power

easily. Don't forget to say each **Wort** as you attach the label.

Now ask yourself, „**Wo ist die Lampe?**" *(dee) (lahm-puh)* **und** point at it while you answer, „**Dort ist die Lampe.**" *(dort)* [there]

Continue on down the list above until you feel comfortable with these new **Wörter.**

❏	**der Appetit** *(ah-peh-teet)*	appetite	
❏	**der April** *(ah-pril)*	April	
❏	**der August** *(ow-goost)*	August	**a**
❏	**das Auto** *(ow-toh)*	car, automobile	
❏	**der Autor** *(ow-tor)*	author	

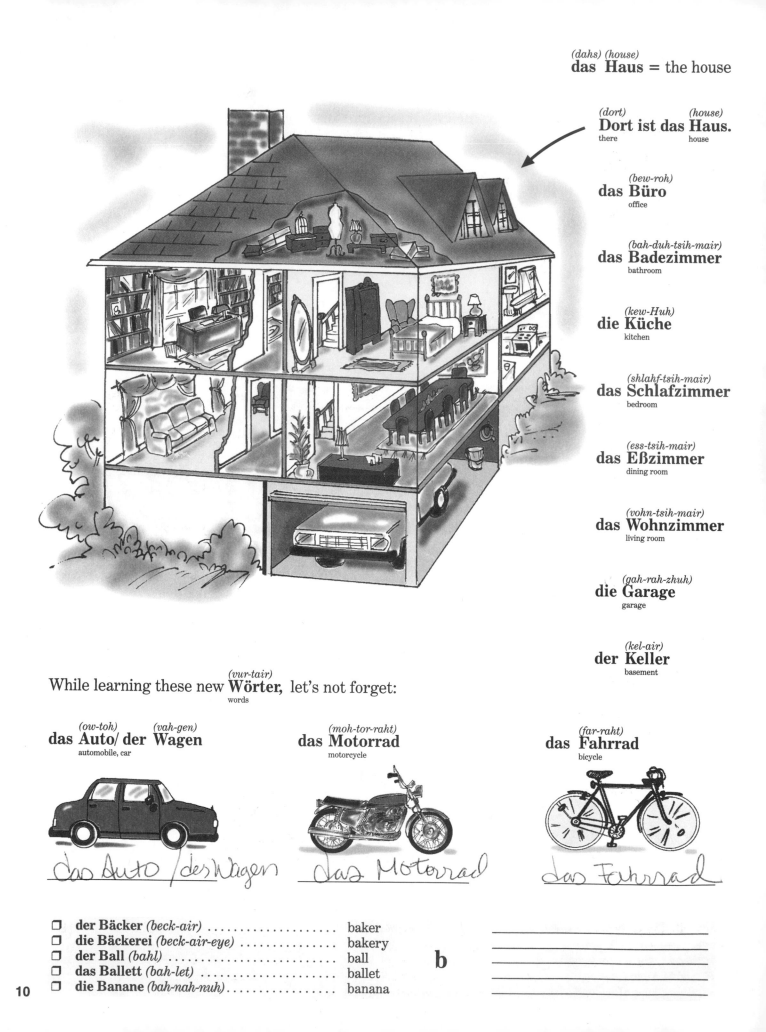

(dahs) (house)
das Haus = the house

(dort) *(house)*
Dort ist das Haus.
there house

(bew-roh)
das Büro
office

(bah-duh-tsih-mair)
das Badezimmer
bathroom

(kew-Huh)
die Küche
kitchen

(shlahf-tsih-mair)
das Schlafzimmer
bedroom

(ess-tsih-mair)
das Eßzimmer
dining room

(vohn-tsih-mair)
das Wohnzimmer
living room

(gah-rah-zhuh)
die Garage
garage

(kel-air)
der Keller
basement

While learning these new **Wörter,** *(vur-tair)* let's not forget:
words

(ow-toh) *(vah-gen)*
das Auto/ der Wagen
automobile, car

das Auto / des Wagen

(moh-tor-raht)
das Motorrad
motorcycle

das Motorrad

(far-raht)
das Fahrrad
bicycle

das Fahrrad

☐ **der Bäcker** *(beck-air)*	baker
☐ **die Bäckerei** *(beck-air-eye)*	bakery
☐ **der Ball** *(bahl)*	ball
☐ **das Ballett** *(bah-let)*	ballet
☐ **die Banane** *(bah-nah-nuh)*	banana

b

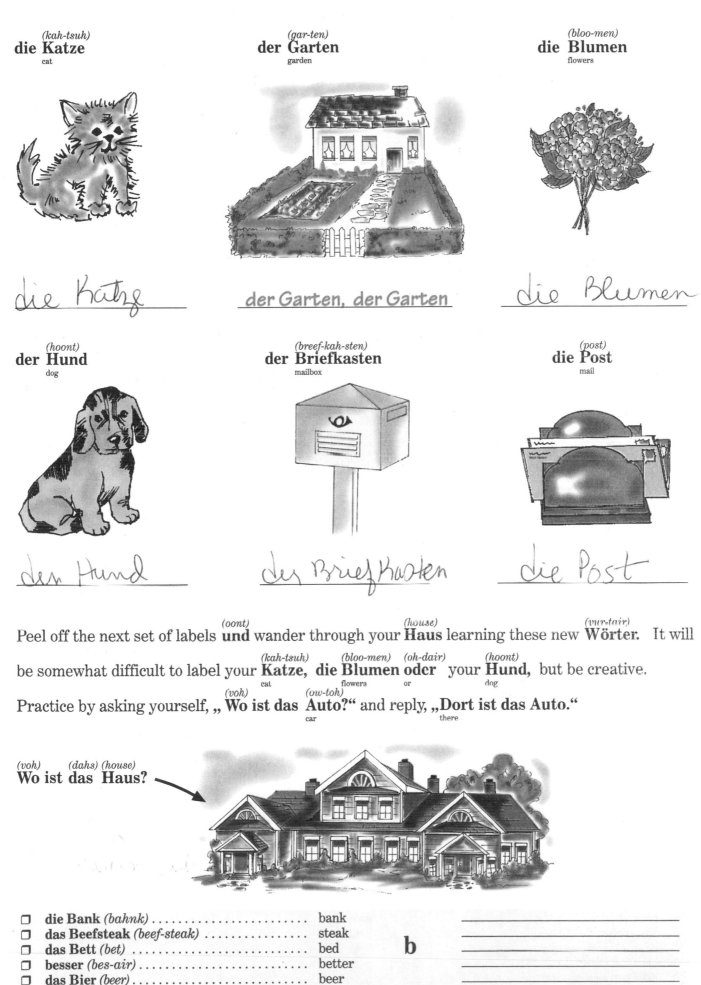

(kah-tsuh)
die Katze
cat

(gar-ten)
der Garten
garden

(bloo-men)
die Blumen
flowers

die Katze

der Garten, der Garten

die Blumen

(hoont)
der Hund
dog

(breef-kah-sten)
der Briefkasten
mailbox

(post)
die Post
mail

der Hund

der Briefkasten

die Post

Peel off the next set of labels **und** wander through your **Haus** *(house)* learning these new **Wörter** *(vur-tair)*. It will

be somewhat difficult to label your **Katze**, **die Blumen oder** your **Hund**, but be creative.
cat   flowers   or   dog

Practice by asking yourself, „**Wo ist das Auto?**" *(voh) (ow-toh)* and reply, „**Dort ist das Auto.**"
car   there

(voh) (dahs) (house)
Wo ist das Haus?

☐	**die Bank** *(bahnk)*	bank	_____
☐	**das Beefsteak** *(beef-steak)*	steak	_____
☐	**das Bett** *(bet)*	bed	**b** _____
☐	**besser** *(bes-air)*	better	_____
☐	**das Bier** *(beer)*	beer	_____

11

Eins, Zwei, Drei!

(eins) one *(tsvy)* two *(dry)* three

Consider for a minute how important numbers are. How could you tell someone your phone number, your address **oder** *(oh-dair)* or your hotel room if you had no numbers? And think of how difficult it would be if you could not understand the time, the price of a **Bier** *(beer)* **oder** the correct bus to take. When practicing **die Nummern** *(noo-mairn)* numbers below, notice the similarities which have been underlined for you between **vier** *(fear)* four **und** **vierzehn,** *(fear-tsayn)* fourteen **drei** *(dry)* three and **dreizehn, und** *(dry-tsayn)* thirteen so on.

0	**null** *(nool)*	*null*
1	**eins** *(eins)*	*eins*
2	**zwei** *(tsvy)*	*zwei*
3	**drei** *(dry)*	*drei*
4	**vier** *(fear)*	*vier*
5	**fünf** *(fewnf)*	*fünf*
6	**sechs** *(zeks)*	*sechs*
7	**sieben** *(zee-ben)*	*sieben, sieben, sieben*
8	**acht** *(ahHt)*	*acht*
9	**neun** *(noyn)*	*neun*
10	**zehn** *(tsayn)*	*zehn*

10	**zehn** *(tsayn)*	*zehn*
11	**elf** *(elf)*	*elf*
12	**zwölf** *(ts-vulf)*	*zwölf*
13	**dreizehn** *(dry-tsayn)*	*dreizehn*
14	**vierzehn** *(fear-tsayn)*	*vierzehn*
15	**fünfzehn** *(fewnf-tsayn)*	*fünfzehn*
16	**sechzehn** *(zeks-tsayn)*	*sechzehn*
17	**siebzehn** *(zeep-tsayn)*	*siebzehn*
18	**achtzehn** *(ahHt-tsayn)*	*achtzehn*
19	**neunzehn** *(noyn-tsayn)*	*neunzehn*
20	**zwanzig** *(tsvahn-tsig)*	*zwanzig*

☑	**blau** *(blau)*	blue	*blau, blau, blau, blau, blau*
☐	**das Boot** *(boht)*	boat	
☐	**braun** *(brown)*	brown	**b**
☐	**bringen** *(bring-en)*	to bring	
☐	**die Butter** *(boo-tair)*	butter	

Use these **Nummern** *(noo-mairn)* *numbers* on a daily basis. Count to yourself **auf Deutsch** *(owf)(doych)* *in German* when you brush your teeth, exercise **oder** *(oh-dair)* commute to work. Fill in the blanks below according to the **Nummern** *(noo-mairn)* *numbers* given in parentheses. Now is also a good time to learn these two very important phrases.

ich *(eeH)* *I* **möchte** *(murk-tuh)* *would like*   *ich möchte ich möchte ich möchte*

wir *(vir)* *we* **möchten** *(murk-ten)* *would like*   *wir möchten wir möchten wir möchten*

Ich *(eeH)* **möchte** *(murk-tuh)* *I would like* _eins_ (1)   **Postkarte.** *(post-kar-tuh)* *postcard*   **Wieviel?** *(vee-feel)* *how many* _eins_ (1)

Ich möchte _sieben_ (7) **Briefmarken.** *(breef-mar-ken)* *stamps*   **Wieviel?** _sieben_ (7)

Ich möchte **acht** (8) **Briefmarken.** *stamps*   **Wieviel?** _acht_ (8)

Ich möchte _fünf_ (5) **Briefmarken.** *stamps*   **Wieviel?** _fünf_ (5)

Wir möchten *(vir)* *we* _neun_ (9) **Postkarten.** *(post-kar-ten)* *postcards*   **Wieviel?** **neun** (9)

Wir möchten *(vir)* _zehn_ (10) **Postkarten.**   **Wieviel?** _zehn_ (10)

Ich möchte *(eeH)* _eins_ (1) **Karte.** *(kar-tuh)* *ticket*   **Wieviel?** _eins_ (1)

Wir möchten _vier_ (4) **Karten.** *(kar-ten)* *tickets*   **Wieviel?** _vier_ (4)

Wir möchten _elf_ (11) **Karten.**   **Wieviel?** *(vee-feel)* _elf_ (11)

Ich möchte _drei_ (3) **Tassen** *(tah-sen)* *cups of* **Tee.** *(tay)* *tea*   **Wieviel?** _drei_ (3)

Wir möchten _vier_ (4) **Glas** *(glahs)* *glasses of* **Wasser.** *(vah-sair)* *water*   *Wieviel* (how many) _vier_ (4)

Deutsch itself has no "C's," so you will see that all of these free **Wörter** come from other languages.

☐ **das Cafe** *(kah-fay)* .... cafe _____
☐ **der Champagner** *(shahm-pahn-yair)* .... champagne _____
☐ **charmant** *(shar-mahnt)* .... charming   **c** _____
☐ **die Chemie** *(shay-mee)* .... chemistry _____

Now see if you can translate the following thoughts into **Deutsch.** *(doych)* German **Die Antworten** *(ahnt-vor-ten)* answers are provided upside down at the bottom of the **Seite.** *(zy-tuh)* page

1. I would like seven postcards.

Ich möchte sieben PostKarte

2. I would like nine stamps.

Ich möchte neun Briefmarken

3. We would like four cups of tea.

Wir möchten vier Tassentee

4. We would like three tickets.

Wir möchten drei Karten.

Review **die Nummern** *(noo-mairn)* 1 through 20. Write out your telephone number, fax number **und** *(oont)* cellular number. Then write out a friend's telephone number and a relative's telephone number.

| (2 | 0 | 6) | 3 | 4 | 0 | — | 4 | 4 | 2 | 2 |

zwei null sechs drie vier null vier vier zwei zwei

(0 1 7) 5 9 6 - 8 3 5 9

null eins sieben fünf neun sechs acht drei fünf neun

(2 6 2) 7 8 3 - 7 2 7 7

zwei sechs zwei sieben acht drei sieben zwei sieben sieben

Die Farben
(dee) (far-ben)
colors

Die Farben *(far-ben)* **sind** *(zint)* the same **in** **Deutschland** *(doych-lahnt)* as they are in the United States — they just have
colors   are   in

different **Namen.** *(nah-men)* You can easily recognize **violett** *(vee-oh-let)* as violet and **purpur** *(poor-poor)* as purple. Let's learn
names

the basic **Farben** *(far-ben)* so when you are invited to someone's **Haus und** *house* you want to bring flowers, you

will be able to order the color you want. Once you've learned **die Farben,** quiz yourself. What

color are your shoes? Your eyes? Your hair? Your house?

(roh-zah)
rosa
pink

(roht)
rot
red

(oh-rahn-zhuh)
orange
orange

(vice)
weiß
white
weiß

(blau)
blau
blue
blau, blau

(grau)
grau
gray
grau

(gelp)
gelb
yellow

(brown)
braun
brown

(grewn)
grün
green
grün

(shvarts)
schwarz
black

(boont)
bunt
multi-colored

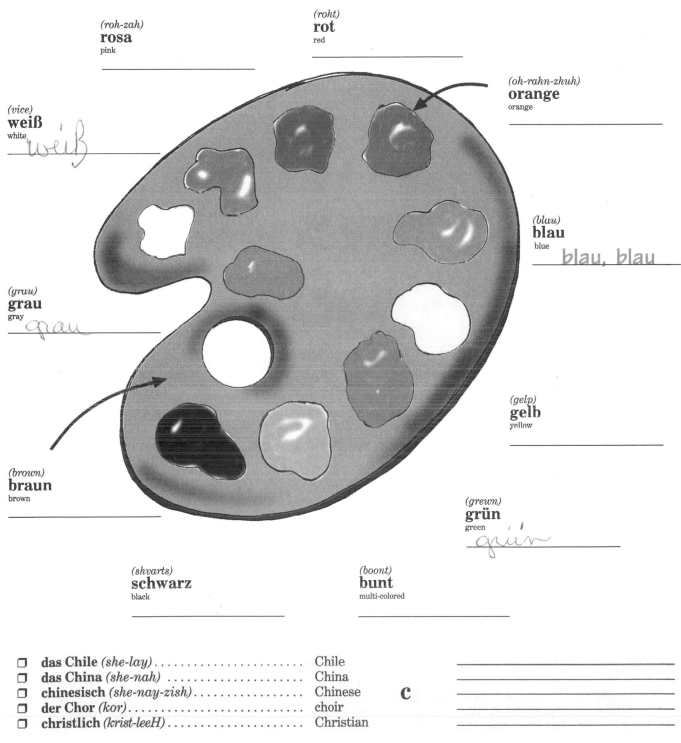

☐ **das Chile** *(she-lay)*	Chile	_____
☐ **das China** *(she-nah)*	China	_____
☐ **chinesisch** *(she-nay-zish)*	Chinese	**c** _____
☐ **der Chor** *(kor)*	choir	_____
☐ **christlich** *(krist-leeH)*	Christian	_____

Peel off the next group of labels **und** proceed to label these **Farben** in your **Haus.** _house_ Identify the

two **oder** three dominant colors in the flags below.
_or_

Germany _____

Switzerland _____

United States _____

Poland _____

Italy _____

The Netherlands _____

United Kingdom _____

Austria _____

Canada _____

France _____

Czech Republic _____

Luxembourg _____

Denmark _____

Belgium _____

You should be able to use your German language skills in some of the above countries as well as

in **Deutschland.** Did you notice that a "**b**" at the end of a word as in „**gelb**" _(gelp)_ can be pronounced as

a "p"?

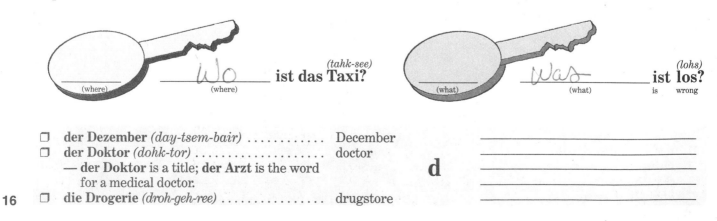

_____ Wo _____ ist das **Taxi?** _(tahk-see)_
(where)   (where)

_____ Was _____ ist **los?** _(lohs)_
(what)   (what)   is   wrong

☐ **der Dezember** _(day-tsem-bair)_ .... December
☐ **der Doktor** _(dohk-tor)_ .... doctor
  — **der Doktor** is a title; **der Arzt** is the word
    for a medical doctor.

d

_____
_____
_____

16 ☐ **die Drogerie** _(droh-geh-ree)_ .... drugstore
_____

(lahm-puh) **die Lampe**	*(ow-toh)* **das Auto**	*(brown)* **braun**	*(beer)* **das Bier**
(zoh-fah) **das Sofa**	*(moh-tor-raht)* **das Motorrad**	*(roht)* **rot**	*(milsh)* **die Milch**
(shtool) **der Stuhl**	*(far-raht)* **das Fahrrad**	*(roh-zah)* **rosa**	*(boo-tair)* **die Butter**
(tep-eeH) **der Teppich**	*(kah-tsuh)* **die Katze**	*(oh-rahn-zhuh)* **orange**	*(zahlts)* **das Salz**
(tish) **der Tisch**	*(gar-ten)* **der Garten**	*(vice)* **weiß**	*(fef-air)* **der Pfeffer**
(tewr) **die Tür**	*(bloo-men)* **die Blumen**	*(gelp)* **gelb**	*(vine-glahs)* **das Weinglas**
(oor) **die Uhr**	*(hoont)* **der Hund**	*(grau)* **grau**	*(glahs)* **das Glas**
(for-hahng) **der Vorhang**	*(breef-kah-sten)* **der Briefkasten**	*(shvarts)* **schwarz**	*(tsy-toong)* **die Zeitung**
(tay-lay-fohn) **das Telefon**	*(post)* **die Post**	*(blau)* **blau**	*(tah-suh)* **die Tasse**
(fehn-stair) **das Fenster**	*(nool)* 0 **null**	*(grewn)* **grün**	*(luh fel)* **der Löffel**
(bilt) **das Bild**	*(eins)* 1 **eins**	*(boont)* **bunt**	*(mes-air)* **das Messer**
(house) **das Haus**	*(tsvy)* 2 **zwei**	*(goo-ten)* *(mor-gen)* **Guten Morgen**	*(zair-vee-et-tuh)* **die Serviette**
(bew-roh) **das Büro**	*(dry)* 3 **drei**	*(goo-ten)* *(tahk)* **Guten Tag**	*(tel-air)* **der Teller**
(bah-duh-tsih-mair) **das Badezimmer**	*(fear)* 4 **vier**	*(goo-ten)* *(ah-bent)* **Guten Abend**	*(gah-bel)* **die Gabel**
(kew-Huh) **die Küche**	*(fewnf)* 5 **fünf**	*(goo-tuh)* *(nahHt)* **Gute Nacht**	*(shrahnk)* **der Schrank**
(shlahf-tsih-mair) **das Schlafzimmer**	*(zeks)* 6 **sechs**	*(owf)* *(vee-dair-zay-en)* **Auf Wiedersehen**	*(tay)* **der Tee**
(ess-tsih-mair) **das Eßzimmer**	*(zee-ben)* 7 **sieben**	*(vee)* *(gate)* *(es)* *(ee-nen)* **Wie geht es Ihnen?**	*(kah-fay)* **der Kaffee**
(vohn-tsih-mair) **das Wohnzimmer**	*(ahHt)* 8 **acht**	*(kewl-shrahnk)* **der Kühlschrank**	*(broht)* **das Brot**
(gah-rah-zhuh) **die Garage**	*(noyn)* 9 **neun**	*(oh-fen)* **der Ofen**	*(bit-tuh)* **bitte**
(kel-air) **der Keller**	*(tsayn)* 10 **zehn**	*(vine)* **der Wein**	*(dahn-kuh)* **danke**

STICKY LABELS

This book has over 150 special sticky labels for you to use as you learn new words. When you are introduced to one of these words, remove the corresponding label from these pages. Be sure to use each of these unique self-adhesive labels by adhering them to a picture, window, lamp, or whatever object they refer to. And yes, they are removable! The sticky labels make learning to speak German much more fun and a lot easier than you ever expected. For example, when you look in the mirror and see the label, say

(dair)   (shpee-gel)
„der Spiegel.“ ⟶
_{mirror}

Don't just say it once, say it again and again. And once you label the refrigerator, you should never again open that door without saying

(kewl-shrahnk)
„der Kühlschrank.“
_{refrigerator}

By using the sticky labels, you not only learn new words, but friends and family learn along with you! The sooner you start, the sooner you can use these labels at home or work.

(dahs) *(gelt)*
Das Geld
money

Before starting this Step, go back and review Step 5. It is important that you can count to

(tsvahn-tsig) zwanzig without looking at **das Buch.** *(booH)* Let's learn the larger **Nummern** *(noo-mairn)* now. After practicing
twenty — book

aloud **die deutschen Nummern** *(dee) (doy-chen)* 10 through 1,000 below, write these **Nummern** in the blanks

provided. Again, notice the similarities (underlined) between numbers such as **vier** *(fear)* (4),

(fear-tsayn) **vierzehn** (14), **und** **vierzig** *(fear-tsig)* (40).

10	*(tsayn)* **zehn**	
20	*(tsvahn-tsig)* **zwanzig**	
30	*(dry-sig)* **dreißig**	
40	*(fear-tsig)* **vierzig**	vierzig, vierzig, vierzig, vierzig, vierzig
50	*(fewnf-tsig)* **fünfzig**	
60	*(zek-tsig)* **sechzig**	
70	*(zeep-tsig)* **siebzig**	
80	*(ahHt-tsig)* **achtzig**	
90	*(noyn-tsig)* **neunzig**	
100	*(hoon-dairt)* **hundert**	
500	*(fewnf-hoon-dairt)* **fünfhundert**	
1.000	*(tau-zent)* **tausend**	

Here are **zwei** *(tsvy)* important phrases to go with all these **Nummern.** Say them out loud over and

over and then write them out twice as many times.

(eeH) *(hah-buh)*
ich habe _____
I have

(vir) *(hah-ben)*
wir haben _____
we have

❑ **das Eis** *(ice)* . . . . ice cream _____
❑ **der Elefant** *(ay-lay-fahnt)* . . . . elephant _____
❑ **das England** *(eng-lahnt)* . . . . England _____
   — where they speak **Englisch** *(eng-lish)*   **e**
❑ **das Europa** *(oy-roh-pah)* . . . . Europe _____

The unit of currency **in Deutschland ist der** *(doych-lahnt)* *(oy-roh)* **Euro,** abbreviated "**€**". Let's learn the various

kinds of **Geldstücke und** *(gelt-shtew-kuh)* **Geldscheine.** *(gelt-shy-nuh)* Always be sure to practice each **Wort** out loud. You
coins   bills

might want to exchange some money **jetzt** *(yets-t)* so that you can familiarize yourself **mit** the various
now   with

types of **Geld.** *(gelt)*
money

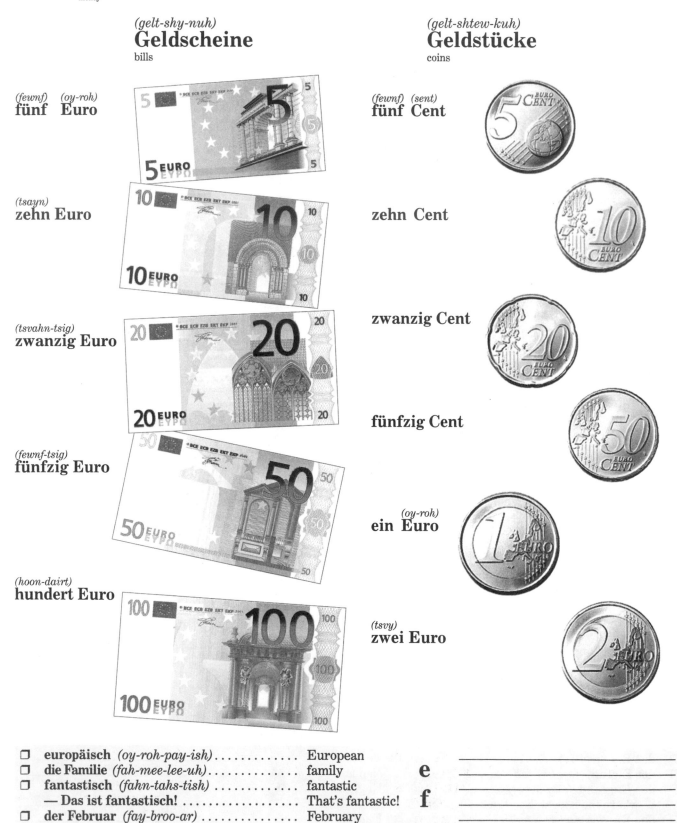

Geldscheine *(gelt-shy-nuh)*
bills

Geldstücke *(gelt-shtew-kuh)*
coins

fünf Euro *(fewnf)* *(oy-roh)*

zehn Euro *(tsayn)*

zwanzig Euro *(tsvahn-tsig)*

fünfzig Euro *(fewnf-tsig)*

hundert Euro *(hoon-dairt)*

fünf Cent *(fewnf)* *(sent)*

zehn Cent

zwanzig Cent

fünfzig Cent

ein Euro *(oy-roh)*

zwei Euro *(tsvy)*

- ❐ **europäisch** *(oy-roh-pay-ish)* .... European
- ❐ **die Familie** *(fah-mee-lee-uh)* .... family
- ❐ **fantastisch** *(fahn-tahs-tish)* .... fantastic
- — **Das ist fantastisch!** .... That's fantastic!
- ❐ **der Februar** *(fay-broo-ar)* .... February

e _____

f _____

Review **die Nummern** **zehn** *(tsayn)* through **tausend** *(tau-zent)* again. **Nun,** *(noon)* how do you say "twenty-two" **oder** *(oh-dair)*
"fifty-three" **auf** *(owf)* **Deutsch?** *(doych)* You basically talk backwards — "two and twenty" *(zwei-und-zwanzig)* **oder** "three and *(drei-und-*
in German
fifty". *(fünfzig)* See if you can say **und** write out **die Nummern** on this **Seite.** *(zy-tuh)* The answers **sind** *(zint)* at the
page   are
bottom of the **Seite.**

1. _____   2. ___dreiundachtzig___
   (25 = 5 + 20)   (83 = 3 + 80)

3. _____   4. _____
   (47 = 7 + 40)   (96 = 6 + 90)

Now, how would you say the following **auf** *(owf)* **Deutsch?** *(doych)*

5. _Ich habe achtzig Euro_
   (I have 80 Euro.)

6. _Wir haben zweiundsiebzig Euro_
   (We have 72 Euro.)

To ask how much something costs **auf Deutsch,** one asks — „**Wieviel** *(vee-feel)* **kostet** *(koh-stet)* **das?**" *(dahs)*

Now you try it. _Wievel kostet das?_
                 (How much does that cost?)

Answer the following questions based on the numbers in parentheses.

7. **Wieviel** *(vee-feel)* **kostet** *(koh-stet)* **das?** *(dahs)* **Es** *(es)* **kostet** *(koh-stet)* ___zehn___ **Euro.** *(oy-roh)*
   costs   that   it   costs   (10)

8. **Wieviel kostet das Bild?** *(bilt)* **Das Bild kostet** ___zwanzig___ **Euro.**
   picture   (20)

9. **Wieviel kostet das Buch?** *(booH)* **Das Buch kostet** *(booH)* ___siebzehn___ **Euro.**
   book   (17)

10. **Wieviel kostet der Film?** *(film)* **Der Film kostet** ___sechs___ **Euro.**
                                                   (6)

(dair) *(kah-len-dair)*
der Kalender
the   calendar

_____

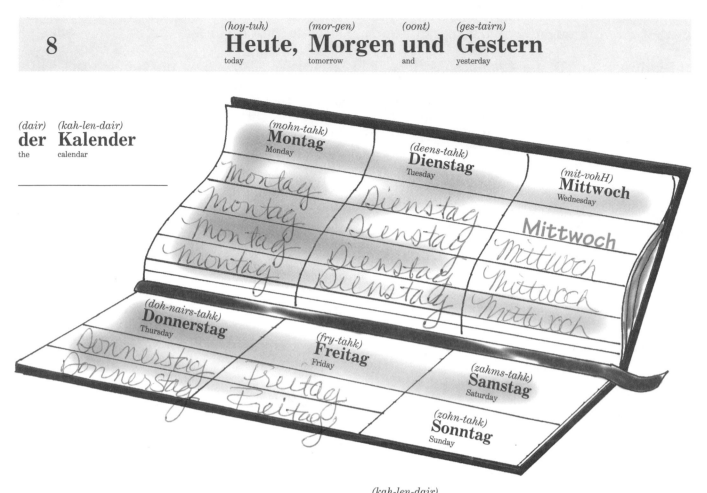

Learn the days of the week by writing them in the *(kah-len-dair)* **Kalender** above **und** then move on to the

(fear) **vier** parts to each *(tahk)* **Tag.**
four   day

(mor-gen)
der Morgen
morning

(nahH-mit-tahk)
der Nachmittag
afternoon

(ah-bent)
der Abend
evening

(nahHt)
die Nacht
night

der Morgen   der Nachmittag   der Abend   die Nacht

☐ **der Film** *(film)*	film	_____
☐ **finden** *(fin-den)*	to find	_____
— Ich finde das Hotelzimmer.		
☐ **der Finger** *(fing-air)*	finger	_____
☐ **der Fisch** *(fish)*	fish	_____

f

Es ist *(zair)* **sehr** important to know the days of the week **und** the various parts of the *(tahk)* **Tag** as well as
very

these *(dry)* *(vur-tair)* **drei Wörter.**
three

(ges-tairn) **gestern** *(hoy-tuh)* **heute** *(mor-gen)* **morgen**

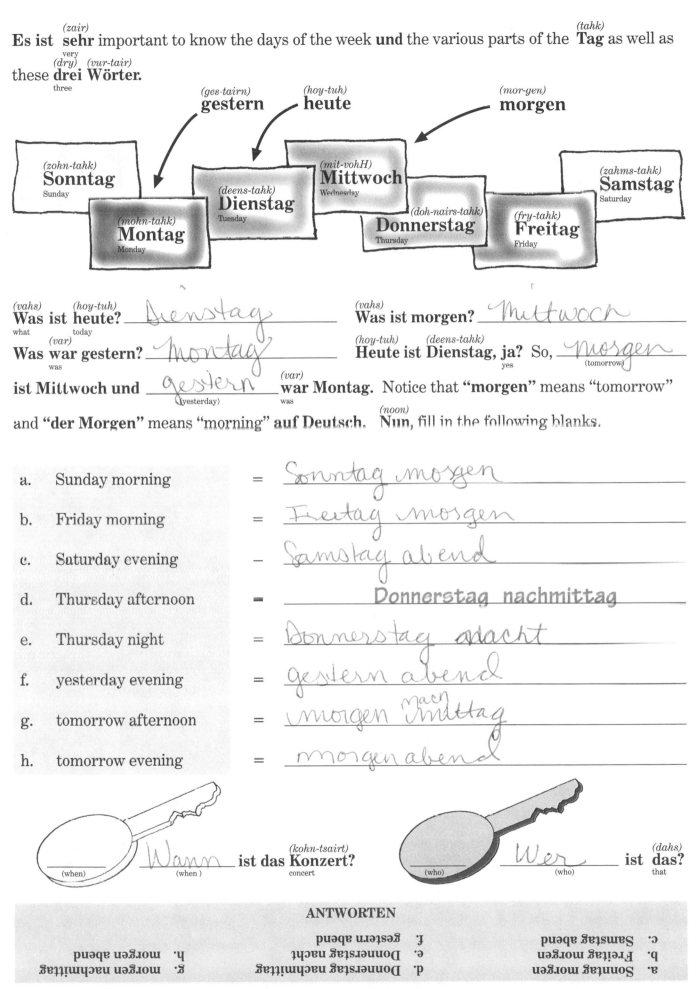

(zohn-tahk) **Sonntag** Sunday

(mohn-tahk) **Montag** Monday

(deens-tahk) **Dienstag** Tuesday

(mit-vohH) **Mittwoch** Wednesday

(doh-nairs-tahk) **Donnerstag** Thursday

(fry-tahk) **Freitag** Friday

(zahms-tahk) **Samstag** Saturday

(vahs) *(hoy-tuh)* **Was ist heute?** _Dienstag_
what today

(vahs) **Was ist morgen?** _Mittwoch_

(var) **Was war gestern?** _Montag_
was

(hoy-tuh) *(deens-tahk)* **Heute ist Dienstag, ja?** So, _morgen_
yes (tomorrow)

ist Mittwoch und _gestern_ *(var)* **war Montag.** Notice that **"morgen"** means "tomorrow"
(yesterday) was

and **"der Morgen"** means "morning" **auf Deutsch.** *(noon)* **Nun,** fill in the following blanks.

a.	Sunday morning	=	Sonntag morgen
b.	Friday morning	=	Freitag morgen
c.	Saturday evening	=	Samstag abend
d.	Thursday afternoon	=	Donnerstag nachmittag
e.	Thursday night	=	Donnerstag nacht
f.	yesterday evening	=	gestern abend
g.	tomorrow afternoon	=	morgen nach mittag
h.	tomorrow evening	=	morgen abend

Wann **ist das** *(kohn-tsairt)* **Konzert?**
(when) (when) concert

Wer **ist** *(dahs)* **das?**
(who) (who) that

ANTWORTEN

a. **Sonntag morgen**
b. **Freitag morgen**
c. **Samstag abend**

d. **Donnerstag nachmittag**
e. **Donnerstag nacht**
f. **gestern abend**

g. **morgen nachmittag**
h. **morgen abend**

23

Knowing the parts of the **Tag** *(tahk)* day will help you to learn the various **deutsche** *(doy-chuh)* greetings below.

Practice these every day until your trip.

(goo-ten) *(mor-gen)*
Guten Morgen _____
good   morning

(goo-ten) *(tahk)*
Guten Tag _____
good   day/hello

(ah-bent)
Guten Abend _____
good   evening

(goo-tuh) *(nahHt)*
Gute Nacht _____
good   night

(owf) *(vee-dair-zay-en)*
Auf Wiedersehen _____
good-bye

Take the next **vier** *(fear)* four labels **und** *(oont)* stick them on the appropriate **Dinge** *(ding-uh)* things in your **Haus.** *(house)* house Make sure

you attach them to the correct items, as they are only **auf Deutsch.** *(owf)* How about the bathroom

mirror **für** *(fewr)* for „**Guten Morgen**"? *(goo-ten)* **Oder** *(oh-dair)* or your alarm clock **für** *(fewr)* „**Gute Nacht**"? *(goo-tuh)* *(nahHt)* Let's not forget,

(vee) *(gate)* *(ee-nen)*
Wie geht es Ihnen? _____
how are you

Now for some „**ja**" *(yah)* yes or „**nein**" *(nine)* no questions –

Are your eyes **blau?**_____   Are your shoes **braun?** *(brown)* _____

Is your favorite color **rot?** *(roht)* _____   Is today **Samstag?**_____

Do you own a **Katze?** *(kah-tsuh)* _____   Do you own a **Hund?** *(hoont)* _____

You **sind** *(zint)* are about one-fourth of your way through this **Buch und es ist** *(booH)* book *(oont)* it is a good time to quickly

review **die Wörter** *(vur-tair)* you **haben** *(hah-ben)* have learned before doing the crossword puzzle on the next **Seite.** *(zy-tuh)* page

(feel) *(shpahs)* *(feel)* *(glewk)*
Viel Spaß und viel Glück!
have fun   much luck

ANTWORTEN TO THE CROSSWORD PUZZLE

ACROSS

1. **Dienstag**
2. **Nachmittag**
3. **Mittwoch**
4. **heute**
5. **Donnerstag**
6. **fünf**
7. **Abend**
8. **dreißig**
9. **wieviel**
10. **Amerika**
11. **sieben**
12. **frei**
13. **Bank**
14. **gestern**
15. **deutsch**
16. **blau**
17. **der / die / das**
18. **sechzig**
19. **rosa**

20. **haben**
21. **Tag**
22. **vier**
23. **gelb**
24. **zwanzig**
25. **gut**
26. **warum**
27. **Büro**
28. **Bier**

DOWN

1. **neun**
2. **Sonntag**
3. **Auto**
4. **Nacht**
5. **Familie**
6. **morgen**
7. **Montag**
8. **Samstag**
9. **weiß**

10. **wer**
11. **elf**
12. **Freitag**
13. **Bus**
14. **kommen**
16. **bunt**
17. **Bild**
18. **eins**
19. **rot**

20. **Tee**
21. **Bett**
22. **vierzig**
23. **grau**
24. **Zug**
25. **grün**
26. **wo**
28. **schwarz**

CROSSWORD PUZZLE (DAS KREUZWORTRÄTSEL)
(kroits-vort-rate-zel)

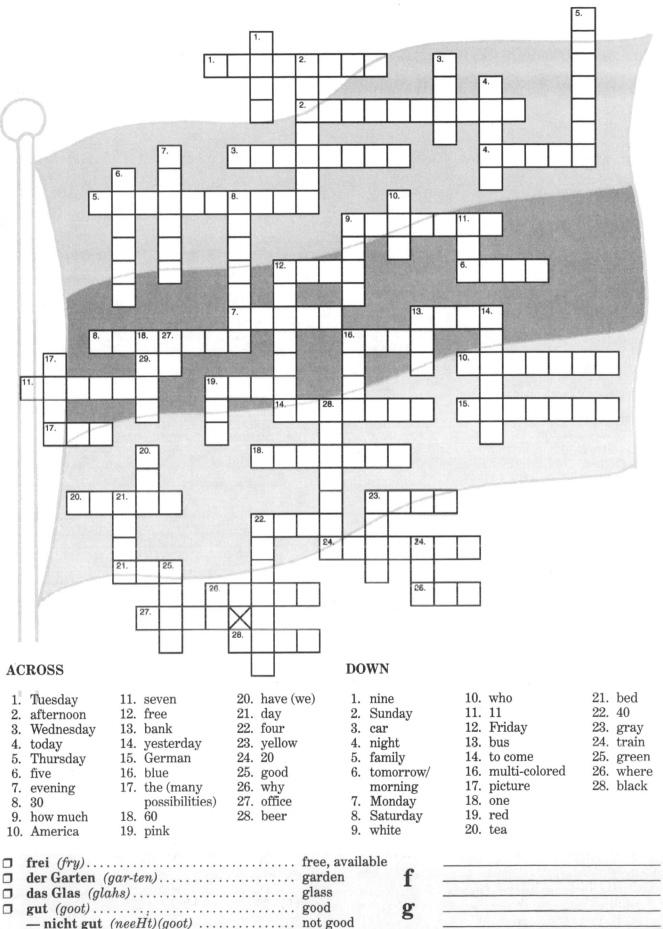

ACROSS

1. Tuesday
2. afternoon
3. Wednesday
4. today
5. Thursday
6. five
7. evening
8. 30
9. how much
10. America
11. seven
12. free
13. bank
14. yesterday
15. German
16. blue
17. the (many possibilities)
18. 60
19. pink
20. have (we)
21. day
22. four
23. yellow
24. 20
25. good
26. why
27. office
28. beer

DOWN

1. nine
2. Sunday
3. car
4. night
5. family
6. tomorrow/ morning
7. Monday
8. Saturday
9. white
10. who
11. 11
12. Friday
13. bus
14. to come
16. multi-colored
17. picture
18. one
19. red
20. tea
21. bed
22. 40
23. gray
24. train
25. green
26. where
28. black

☐ **frei** *(fry)* . . . . free, available
☐ **der Garten** *(gar-ten)* . . . . garden
☐ **das Glas** *(glahs)* . . . . glass **f** _____
☐ **gut** *(goot)* . . . . good _____
— **nicht gut** *(neeHt)(goot)* . . . . not good **g** _____

9   *(in)* *(ahn)* *(owf)*
In, an, auf ...
in   on   on top of

(doy-chuh)
Deutsche prepositions (words like "in," "on," "through" and "next to") **sind** *(zint)* easy to learn **und** *(oont)*
are

they allow you to be precise **mit** *(mit)* a minimum of effort. Instead of having to point **sechs** *(zeks)* times
with

at a piece of yummy pastry you would like, you can explain precisely which one you want by

saying **es ist** behind, in front of, next to **oder** *(oh-dair)* under the piece of pastry that the salesperson is
it   is

starting to pick up. Let's learn some of these little **Wörter.** *(vur-tair)*

(oon-tair) **unter**_____ under	*(in)* **in**_____ into / in
(ew-bair) **über**_____ over	*(for)* **vor**_____ in front of
(owf) **auf**_____ on top of (horizontal surfaces)	*(hin-tair)* **hinter**_____ behind
(nay-ben) **neben**_____ next to	*(ows)* **aus**_____ out of / from
(ahn) **an**_____ on / upon (vertical surfaces)	*(tsvih-shen)* **zwischen**_____ between

Fill in the blanks on the next **Seite** *(zy-tuh)* with the correct prepositions from those you **haben** *(hah-ben)* just

learned.

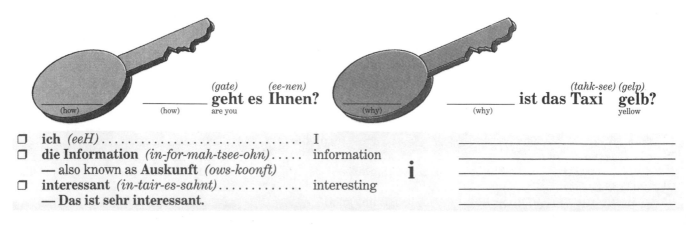

_____ **geht es Ihnen?** *(gate)* *(ee-nen)*
(how)   (how)   are you

_____ **ist das Taxi gelb?** *(tahk-see)* *(gelp)*
(why)   (why)   yellow

❑ **ich** *(eeH)* I
❑ **die Information** *(in-for-mah-tsee-ohn)* ..... information
— also known as **Auskunft** *(ows-koonft)*
❑ **interessant** *(in-tair-es-sahnt)* .... interesting
— Das ist sehr interessant.

i

_____
_____
_____
_____

Der *(koo-Hen)* **Kuchen ist** _____ **dem Tisch.**
pastry/cake *(on)* *table*

Der Hund ist *(hoont)* _____ **dem Tisch.**
dog *(under)* *table*

Der Arzt ist *(arts-t)* _____ **dem guten Hotel.**
doctor *(in)* *good* *(goo-ten)*

Wo ist der Arzt? *(voh)* *(arts-t)* _____

Der Mann ist *(mahn)* _____ **dem Hotel.**
man *(in front of)*

Wo ist der Mann? *(mahn)* _____

Das Telefon ist *(tay-lay-fohn)* _____ **dem Bild.**
telephone *(next to)* *picture* *(bilt)*

Wo ist das Telefon? *(voh)* *(dahs)* *(tay-lay-fohn)* _____

Nun, *(noon)* fill in each blank on the picture below with the best possible one of these little **Wörter.**
now

Do you recognize **das Heidelberger** *(hi-del-bair-gair)* **Schloß** *(shlohs)* below?
Heidelberg *castle*

_____ *(over)*

_____ *(on top of)*

_____ *(next to)*

_____ *(between)*

_____ *(behind)*

_____ *(in front of)*

_____ *(under)*

☐ **das Institut** *(in-stee-toot)* .... institution
☐ **das Italien** *(ee-tah-lee-en)* .... Italy
— where they speak **Italienisch** *(ee-tah-lee-ay-nish)*
☐ **ja** *(yah)* .... yes
☐ **die Jacke** *(yah-kuh)* .... jacket

i _____

j _____
_____
_____

27

(yah-noo-ar) *(fay-broo-ar)* *(merts)*
Januar, Februar, März
January   February   March

You **haben** learned the days of the **Woche,** so now **es ist** time to learn **die Monate** of the **Jahr**
(hah-ben) *(voh-Huh)* week *(moh-nah-tuh)* months *(yar)* year
und all the different kinds of **Wetter.**
(oont) *(vet-tair)* weather

When someone asks, „ **Wie ist das Wetter heute?**" you have a variety of answers. Let's learn
(vee) *(vet-tair)* *(hoy-tuh)*
how   is   weather   today

them but first, does this sound familiar?

(dry-sig) *(haht)* *(zep-tem-bair)* *(ah-pril)* *(yoo-nee)* *(noh-vem-bair)*
Dreißig Tage hat September, April, Juni und November...
has

☐ **das Jahr** *(yar)* .... year _____
☐ **der Januar** *(yah-noo-ar)* .... January _____
☐ **das Japan** *(yah-pahn)* .... Japan   **j** _____
— where they speak **Japanisch** *(yah-pah-nish)* _____
☐ **das Journal** *(zhoor-nahl)* .... journal, magazine _____

(vee) *(vet-tair)* *(hoy-tuh)*
Wie ist das Wetter heute? _____
today

(shnight) *(yah-noo-ar)*
Es schneit im Januar. _____
it snows in

(owH) *(fay-broo-ar)*
Es schneit auch im Februar. _____
also

(rayg-net) *(merts)*
Es regnet im März. _____
it rains

(ah-pril)
Es regnet auch im April. _____

(vin-dig) *(my)*
Es ist windig im Mai. _____
windy

(varm) *(yoo-nee)*
Es ist warm im Juni. _____
warm

(shuhn) *(yoo-lee)*
Es ist schön im Juli. _____
pretty

(hice) *(ow-goost)*
Es ist heiß im August. _____
hot

(nay-blig) *(zep-tem-bair)*
Es ist neblig im September. _____
foggy

(kewl) *(ohk-toh-bair)*
Es ist kühl im Oktober. _____
cool

(schlehHt) *(noh-vom bair)*
Es ist schlecht im November. _____
bad

(kahlt) *(day-tsem-bair)*
Es ist kalt im Dezember. _____
cold

(vee) *(vet-tair)*
Wie ist das Wetter im Februar? _____
how

Wie ist das Wetter im April? _____ *Es regnet im April. Es regnet im April.*

Wie ist das Wetter im Mai? _____

Wie ist das Wetter im August? _____

☐ **der Juli** *(yoo-lee)* . . . . July
☐ **der Juni** *(yoo-nee)* . . . . June
　　Notice how often **Englisch** "c" becomes "k" **auf Deutsch.**
☐ **der Kaffee** *(kah-fay)* . . . . coffee
☐ **das Kaffeehaus** *(kay-fay-house)* . . . . coffee house

j _____

k _____
_____

29

Nun für *(fewr)* the seasons of the **Jahr** *(yar)* ...
year

der Winter *(vin-tair)*
winter

der Sommer *(zoh-mair)*
summer

der Herbst *(hairp-st)*
autumn

der Frühling *(frew-ling)*
spring

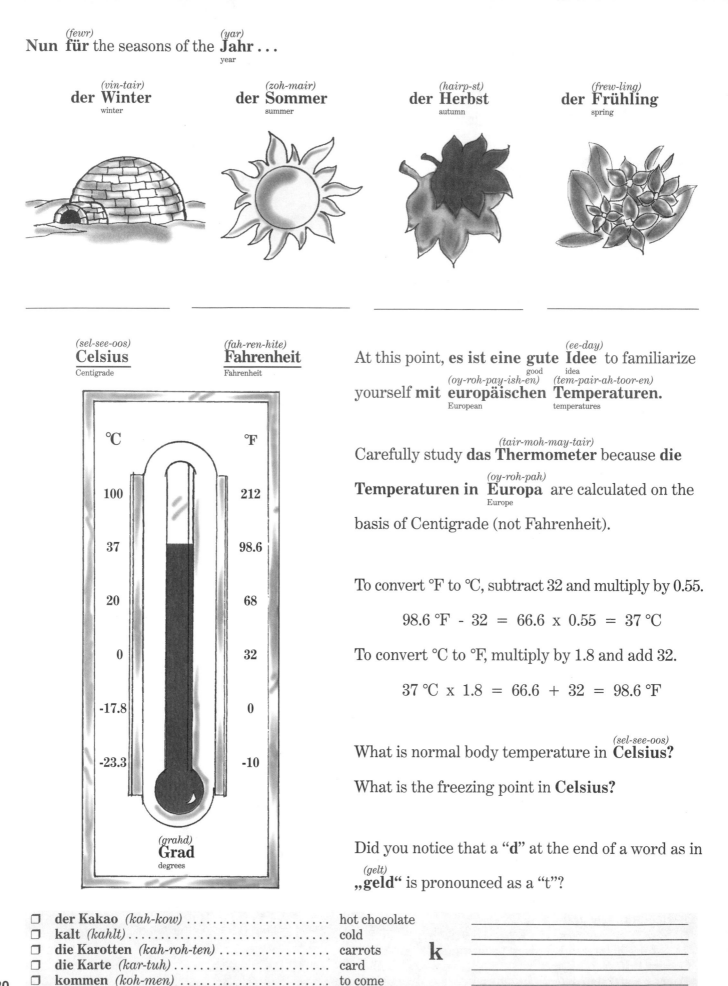

Celsius *(sel-see-oos)*
Centigrade

Fahrenheit *(fah-ren-hite)*
Fahrenheit

°C		°F
100		212
37		98.6
20		68
0		32
-17.8		0
-23.3		-10

Grad *(grahd)*
degrees

At this point, **es ist eine gute Idee** *(ee-day)* to familiarize
good   idea

yourself **mit europäischen Temperaturen.** *(oy-roh-pay-ish-en)* *(tem-pair-ah-toor-en)*
European   temperatures

Carefully study **das Thermometer** *(tair-moh-may-tair)* because **die**

Temperaturen in Europa *(oy-roh-pah)* are calculated on the
Europe

basis of Centigrade (not Fahrenheit).

To convert °F to °C, subtract 32 and multiply by 0.55.

$$98.6 \text{ °F} - 32 = 66.6 \times 0.55 = 37 \text{ °C}$$

To convert °C to °F, multiply by 1.8 and add 32.

$$37 \text{ °C} \times 1.8 = 66.6 + 32 = 98.6 \text{ °F}$$

What is normal body temperature in **Celsius?** *(sel-see-oos)*

What is the freezing point in **Celsius?**

Did you notice that a "**d**" at the end of a word as in

„**geld**" *(gelt)* is pronounced as a "**t**"?

☐ **der Kakao** *(kah-kow)* .... hot chocolate
☐ **kalt** *(kahlt)* .... cold
☐ **die Karotten** *(kah-roh-ten)* .... carrots
☐ **die Karte** *(kar-tuh)* .... card
☐ **kommen** *(koh-men)* .... to come

k

Just as we have the three "R's" **auf Englisch, auf Deutsch** there are the three "K's" which help

us to understand some of the basics of German life. Study the family tree below.

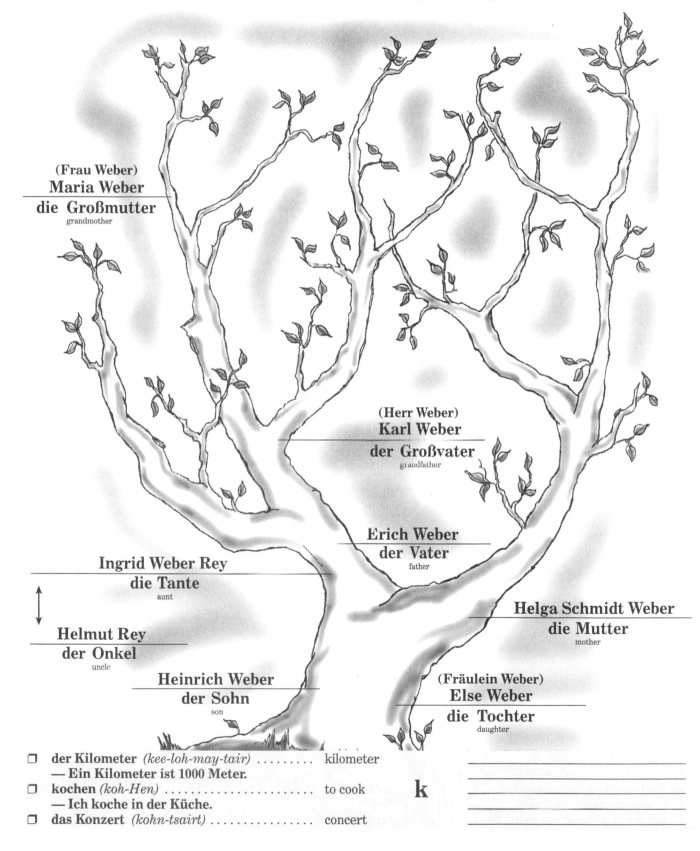

(Frau Weber)
Maria Weber
die Großmutter
grandmother

(Herr Weber)
Karl Weber
der Großvater
grandfather

Erich Weber
der Vater
father

Ingrid Weber Rey
die Tante
aunt

Helga Schmidt Weber
die Mutter
mother

Helmut Rey
der Onkel
uncle

Heinrich Weber
der Sohn
son

(Fräulein Weber)
Else Weber
die Tochter
daughter

☐ **der Kilometer** *(kee-loh-may-tair)* . . . . kilometer
 — **Ein Kilometer ist 1000 Meter.**
☐ **kochen** *(koh-Hen)* . . . . to cook
 — **Ich koche in der Küche.**
☐ **das Konzert** *(kohn-tsairt)* . . . . concert

k

_____
_____
_____
_____

31

Let's learn how to identify **die Familie** _(fah-mee-lee-uh)_ by **Name** _(nah-muh)_. Study the following examples carefully.
family   name

(vee) (hi-sen) (zee)
Wie heißen Sie?_____
what is your name/how are you called

(eeH) (hi-suh)
Ich heiße_____
my name is/I am called   (your name)

(el-tairn)
die Eltern
_____
parents

(fah-tair)
der Vater _____
father

(vee) (heist) (fah-tair)
Wie heißt der Vater?_____
how is called father

(moo-tair)
die Mutter _____
mother

(dee) (moo-tair)
Wie heißt die Mutter?_____
how   mother

(kin-dair)
die Kinder
children

(zohn) _(tohH-tair)_
Der Sohn und die Tochter sind

(broo-dair) _(shves-tair)_
auch Bruder und Schwester!
brother   sister

(zohn)
der Sohn _____
son

(vee) (dair)
Wie heißt der Sohn?_____
son

(tohH-tair)
die Tochter _____
daughter

(heist) (tohH-tair)
Wie heißt die Tochter? _____
daughter

(fair-vahn-ten)
die Verwandten
relatives

(grohs-fah-tair)
der Großvater_____
grandfather

(dair) (grohs-fah-tair)
Wie heißt der Großvater? _____
grandfather

(grohs-moo-tair)
die Großmutter_____
grandmother

(heist)
Wie heißt die Großmutter? _____
grandmother

Now you ask —

_____
(How are you called?/What is your name?)

And answer —

_____
(My name is . . .)

❐	**kosten** _(koh-sten)_	to cost	_____
	— **Es kostet 20 Mark.**		_____
❐	**das Kotelett** _(koh-teh-let)_............	cutlet	**k**
❐	**kühl** _(kewl)_	cool	_____
❐	**der Kühlschrank** _(kewl-shrahnk)_	refrigerator	

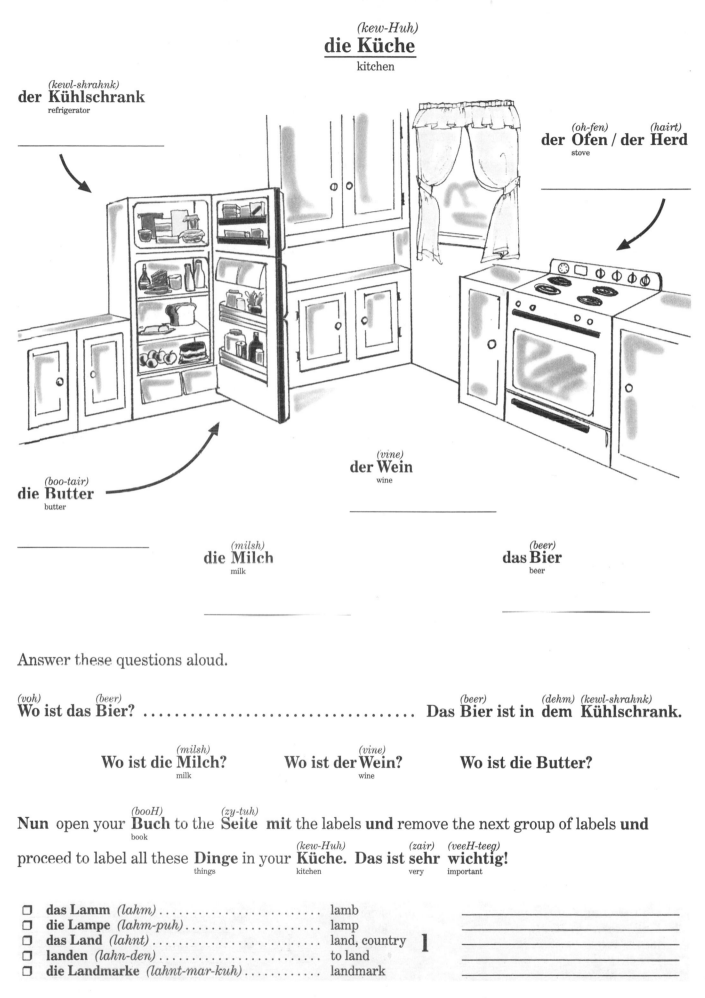

(kew-Huh)
die Küche
kitchen

(kewl-shrahnk)
der Kühlschrank
refrigerator

_____

(oh-fen)   *(hairt)*
der Ofen / der Herd
stove

_____

(boo-tair)
die Butter
butter

_____

(vine)
der Wein
wine

_____

(milsh)
die Milch
milk

_____

(beer)
das Bier
beer

_____

Answer these questions aloud.

(voh)   *(beer)*
Wo ist das Bier? .... *(beer)* *(dehm)* *(kewl-shrahnk)* **Das Bier ist in dem Kühlschrank.**

(milsh)
Wo ist die Milch?
milk

(vine)
Wo ist der Wein?
wine

Wo ist die Butter?

(booH)   *(zy-tuh)*
Nun open your **Buch** to the **Seite** **mit** the labels **und** remove the next group of labels **und**
book

(kew-Huh) *(zair)* *(veeH-teeg)*
proceed to label all these **Dinge** in your **Küche. Das ist sehr wichtig!**
things   kitchen   very   important

☐	**das Lamm** *(lahm)*	lamb	_____
☐	**die Lampe** *(lahm-puh)*	lamp	_____
☐	**das Land** *(lahnt)*	land, country	_____
☐	**landen** *(lahn-den)*	to land	_____
☐	**die Landmarke** *(lahnt-mar-kuh)*	landmark	_____

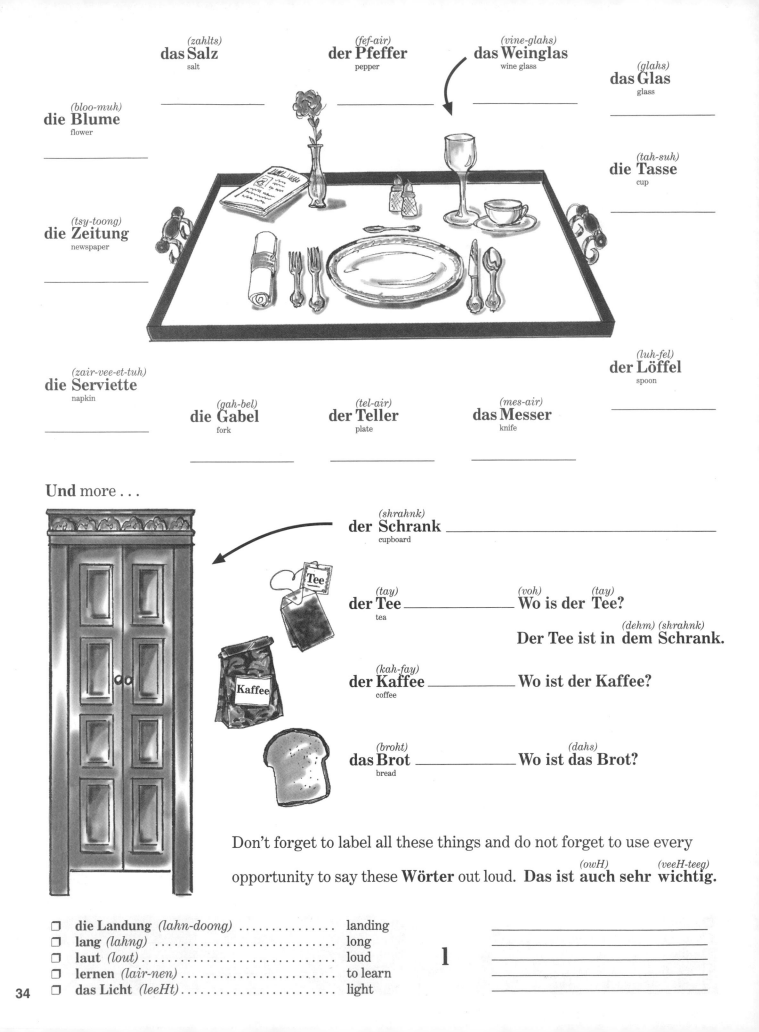

(zahlts)
das **Salz**
salt

(fef-air)
der **Pfeffer**
pepper

(vine-glahs)
das **Weinglas**
wine glass

(glahs)
das **Glas**
glass

(bloo-muh)
die **Blume**
flower

(tah-suh)
die **Tasse**
cup

(tsy-toong)
die **Zeitung**
newspaper

(luh-fel)
der **Löffel**
spoon

(zair-vee-et-tuh)
die **Serviette**
napkin

(gah-bel)
die **Gabel**
fork

(tel-air)
der **Teller**
plate

(mes-air)
das **Messer**
knife

Und more . . .

(shrahnk)
der **Schrank** _____
cupboard

(tay)
der **Tee** _____
tea

(voh) *(tay)*
Wo is der Tee?

(dehm) (shrahnk)
Der Tee ist in dem Schrank.

(kah-fay)
der **Kaffee** _____
coffee

Wo ist der Kaffee?

(broht)
das **Brot** _____
bread

(dahs)
Wo ist das Brot?

Don't forget to label all these things and do not forget to use every

opportunity to say these **Wörter** out loud. **Das ist auch sehr wichtig.**
(owH) *(veeH-teeg)*

☐ **die Landung** *(lahn-doong)* . . . . landing
☐ **lang** *(lahng)* . . . . long
☐ **laut** *(lout)* . . . . loud
☐ **lernen** *(lair-nen)* . . . . to learn
☐ **das Licht** *(leeHt)* . . . . light

1

(ent-shool-dee-goong) **Entschuldigung**	*(breef)* **der Brief**	*(day-oh)* **das Deo**	*(shorts)* **die Shorts**
(kly-dair-shrahnk) **der Kleiderschrank**	*(breef-mar-kuh)* **die Briefmarke**	*(kahm)* **der Kamm**	*(tee-shirt)* **das T-shirt**
(bet) **das Bett**	*(post-kar-tuh)* **die Postkarte**	*(ray-gen-mahn-tel)* **der Regenmantel**	*(oon-tair-hoh-zuh)* **die Unterhose**
(kohpf-kiss-en) **das Kopfkissen**	*(pahs)* **der Paß**	*(ray-gen-shirm)* **der Regenschirm**	*(oon-tair-hemt)* **das Unterhemd**
(bet-deck-uh) **die Bettdecke**	*(kar-tuh)* **die Karte**	*(mahn-tel)* **der Mantel**	*(klite)* **das Kleid**
(veck-air) **der Wecker**	*(koh-fair)* **der Koffer**	*(hahnt-shoo-uh)* **die Handschuhe**	*(bloo-zuh)* **die Bluse**
(shpee-gel) **der Spiegel**	*(hahnt-tah-shuh)* **die Handtasche**	*(hoot)* **der Hut**	*(rohk)* **der Rock**
(vahsh-beck-en) **das Waschbecken**	*(breef-tah-shuh)* **die Brieftasche**	*(shtee-fel)* **die Stiefel**	*(poo-lee)* **der Pulli**
(tooH) **das Tuch**	*(gelt)* **das Geld**	*(shoo-uh)* **die Schuhe**	*(oon-tair-rohk)* **der Unterrock**
(toy-let-tuh) **die Toilette**	*(kray-deet-kar-ten)* **die Kreditkarten**	*(ten-is-shoo-uh)* **die Tennisschuhe**	*(bay-hah)* **der BH**
(doosh-uh) **die Dusche**	*(ry-zuh-shecks)* **die Reiseschecks**	*(ahn-tsook)* **der Anzug**	*(oon-tair-hoh-zuh)* **die Unterhose**
(bly-shtift) **der Bleistift**	*(kah-mair-ah)* **die Kamera**	*(krah-vah-tuh)* **die Krawatte**	*(zoh-ken)* **die Socken**
(fairn-zay-air) **der Fernseher**	*(film)* **der Film**	*(hemt)* **das Hemd**	*(shtroomf-hoh-zuh)* **die Strumpfhose**
(koo-lee) **der Kuli**	*(bah-duh-ahn-tsook)* **der Badeanzug**	*(tah-shen-tooH)* **das Taschentuch**	*(shlahf-ahn-tsook)* **der Schlafanzug**
(booH) **das Buch**	*(zahn-dah-len)* **die Sandalen**	*(yah-kuh)* **die Jacke**	*(nahHt-hemt)* **das Nachthemd**
(kohm-pyoo-tair) **der Computer**	*(zoh-nen-bril-luh)* **die Sonnenbrille**	*(hoh-zuh)* **die Hose**	*(bah-duh-mahn-tel)* **der Bademantel**
(bril-luh) **die Brille**	*(tsahn-bewr-stuh)* **die Zahnbürste**	*(jeans)* **die Jeans**	*(house-shoo-uh)* **die Hausschuhe**
(pah-peer) **das Papier**	*(tsahn-pah-stuh)* **die Zahnpaste**	*(eeH) (koh-muh) (ows)* **Ich komme aus** _____.	
(pah-peer-korp) **der Papierkorb**	*(zy-fuh)* **die Seife**	*(eeH) (murk-tuh) (doych) (lair-nen)* **Ich möchte Deutsch lernen.**	
(tsight-shrift) **die Zeitschrift**	*(rah-zeer-mes-air)* **das Rasiermesser**	*(eeH) (hi-suh)* **Ich heiße** _____.	

PLUS...

This book includes a number of other innovative features unique to the *"10 minutes a day®"* series. At the back of this book, you will find twelve pages of flash cards. Cut them out and flip through them at least once a day.

On pages 116, 117 and 118 you will find a beverage guide and a menu guide. Don't wait until your trip to use them. Clip out the menu guide and use it tonight at the dinner table. Take them both with you the next time you dine at your favorite German restaurant.

By using the special features in this book, you will be speaking German before you know it.

(feel) *(shpahs)*
Viel Spaß!
have fun

(kir-Huh)
die Kirche
church

In Deutschland there is not the wide variety of **Religionen** *(ray-lee-gee-ohn-en)* that **wir** *(vir)* **finden** *(fin-den)* **hier in** *(here)*
religions we find

(ah-mair-ih-kah)
Amerika. A person is usually one of the following.

(kah-toh-lish)
1. **katholisch** _____
Catholic

(ay-vahn-gay-lish)
2. **evangelisch** _____
Protestant

(yew-dish)
3. **jüdisch** _____
Jewish

(mohz-lem)
4. **Moslem** _____
Moslem

(here) *(eye-nuh)* *(kir-Huh)* *(doych-lahnt)*
Hier ist eine Kirche in Deutschland.
here

(kah-toh-lish-uh)
Ist das eine katholische Kirche?

(ay-vahn-gay-lish-uh)
Ist das eine evangelische Kirche?

(noy-uh)
Ist das eine neue Kirche?
new

(ahl-tuh)
Ist das eine alte Kirche?
old

Nun, let's learn how to say "I am" **auf Deutsch:** **ich bin** *(eeH)* *(bin)* _____
I am

Remember to breath hard when you say „**ich**." *(eeH)* Test yourself — write each sentence on the

next page for more practice. Add your own personal variations as well.

Note that to use a feminine form of many words **auf Deutsch,** all you *generally* need to do is

add an "in." This will sometimes vary the pronounciation slightly.

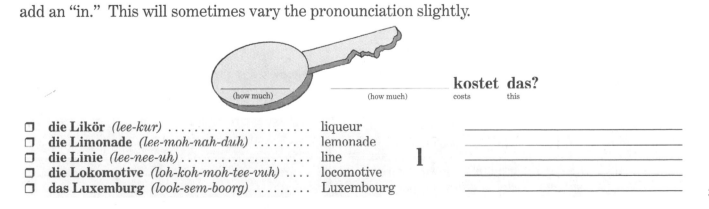

_____ **kostet das?**
(how much) (how much) costs this

1

☐ **die Likör** *(lee-kur)* . . . . liqueur _____
☐ **die Limonade** *(lee-moh-nah-duh)* . . . . lemonade _____
☐ **die Linie** *(lee-nee-uh)* . . . . line _____
☐ **die Lokomotive** *(loh-koh-moh-tee-vuh)* . . . . locomotive _____
☐ **das Luxemburg** *(look-sem-boorg)* . . . . Luxembourg _____

Ich bin katholisch. *(kah-toh-lish)* _____ Ich bin evangelisch. *(ay-vahn-gay-lish)* _____
I am Catholic

Ich bin jüdisch. *(yew-dish)* _____ Ich bin Moslem. *(mohz-lem)* _____
Jewish

Ich bin Amerikaner. *(ah-mair-ih-kahn-air)* _____ Ich bin Amerikanerin. *(ah-mair-ih-kahn-air-in)* _____
American (♂) American (♀)

Ich bin in der Kirche. *(kir-Huh)* _____ Ich bin in Europa. *(oy-roh-pah)* _____
I am in church

Ich bin in Deutschland. *(doych-lahnt)* _____ Ich bin in dem Restaurant. *(dehm) (res-toh-rahnt)* _____

Ich bin Engländer. *(eng-len-dair)* _____ Ich bin in dem Hotel. *(dehm)* _____

Ich bin Kanadier. *(kah-nah-dyair)* _____ Ich bin Kanadierin. *(kah-nah-dyair-in)* _____
Canadian (♂) Canadian (♀)

To negate any of these statements, simply add **"nicht"** *(neeHt)* after the verb.
not

Ich bin **nicht** katholisch. *(neeHt)* _____ Ich bin **nicht** Amerikaner. _____
I am not I am not

Go through and drill all the above sentences again but with „**nicht.**" *(neeHt)*

Nun, take a piece of paper. Our **Familie** *(fah-mee-lee-uh)* from earlier had a reunion. Identify everyone below by writing **das richtige deutsche Wort** *(reeH-tee-guh)* for each person — **die Mutter, den Onkel** *(moo-tair)* *(ohn-kel)* and so on. Don't forget **den Hund!** *(hoont)*
correct

❏ **der Mai** *(my)*	May		_____
❏ **der Mann** *(mahn)*	man		_____
❏ **der Markt** *(markt)*	market	**m**	_____
— usually an open-air market in the town square			_____
❏ **die Marmelade** *(mar-meh-lah-duh)*	marmalade, jam		_____

You have already used *(tsvy)* **zwei** very important verbs: **ich möchte** *(murk-tuh)* and **ich habe** *(hah-buh)*. Although you
I   would like   I   have
might be able to get by with only these verbs, let's assume you want to do better. First, a quick review.

How do you say "**I**" **auf Deutsch?** *(doych)* _____

How do you say "**we**" **auf Deutsch?** _____

Compare these *(tsvy)* **zwei** charts very carefully **und** learn these *(zee-ben)* **sieben Wörter** now.
two   seven

I	=	**ich** *(eeH)*	_____
he	=	**er** *(wir)*	_____
she	=	**sie** *(zee)*	_____
it	=	**es** *(es)*	_____

we	=	**wir** *(vir)*	_____
you	=	**Sie** *(zee)*	_____
they	=	**sie** *(zee)*	_____

Not too hard, is it? Draw lines between the matching **englische und deutsche** *(vur tair)* **Wörter** below to see if you can keep these **Wörter** straight in your mind.

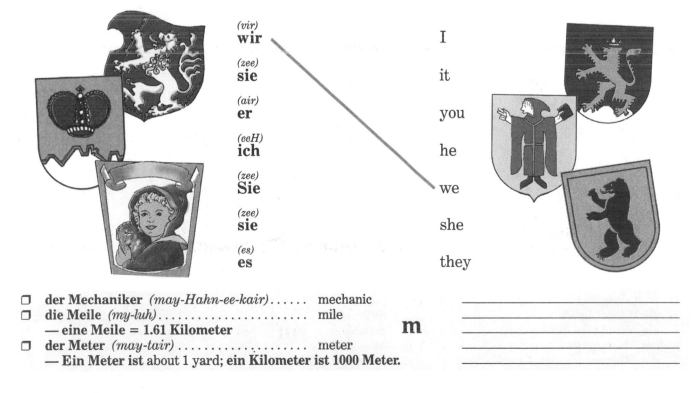

(vir) **wir**	I
(zee) **sie**	it
(air) **er**	you
(eeH) **ich**	he
(zee) **Sie**	we
(zee) **sie**	she
(es) **es**	they

□ **der Mechaniker** *(may-Hahn-ee-kair)* . . . . . . mechanic
□ **die Meile** *(my-luh)* . . . . mile
   — **eine Meile = 1.61 Kilometer**   **m**
□ **der Meter** *(may-tair)* . . . . meter
   — **Ein Meter ist about 1 yard; ein Kilometer ist 1000 Meter.**

_____
_____
_____
_____

Nun close **das Buch und** write out both columns of this practice on **ein Stück Papier.** *(shtewk)* *(pah-peer)* piece (of) paper How did **Sie** *(zee)* do? **Gut oder schlecht?** *(goot)* well *(shlehHt)* oder *(shlehHt)* poorly **Nun** that **Sie** *(zee)* know these **Wörter,** **Sie** *(zee)* you can say almost anything **auf Deutsch** with one basic formula: the "plug-in" formula.

To demonstrate, let's take **sechs** *(zeks)* six basic **und** practical verbs **und** see how the "plug-in" formula works. Write the verbs in the blanks after **Sie** *(zee)* you **haben** *(hah-ben)* have practiced saying them out loud many times.

(koh-men) **kommen** to come	_____	*(gay-en)* **gehen** to go	_____
(hah-ben) **haben** to have	*haben, haben, haben*	*(lair-nen)* **lernen** to learn	_____
(brow-Hen) **brauchen** to need	_____	*(murk-ten)* **möchten** would like	_____

Besides the familiar words already circled, can **Sie** *(zee)* find the above verbs in the puzzle below? When **Sie** *(zee)* find them, write them in the blanks to the right.

P	W	O	M	M	A	H	D	E	R	H
A	A	C	N	P	C	W	A	S	E	A
B	R	A	U	C	H	E	N	B	S	B
L	U	R	S	W	E	E	B	G	E	I
E	M	M	E	K	O	M	M	E	N	N
M	Ö	C	H	T	E	N	M	H	R	E
V	I	N	I	L	R	B	D	E	I	R
L	E	R	N	E	N	L	E	N	H	T

1. _____

2. _____

3. _____

4. _____

5. _____

6. _____

❏	**mehr** *(mair)*	. . . .	more
❏	**die Milch** *(milsh)*	. . . .	milk
❏	**die Mitte** *(mit-tuh)*	. . . .	middle
❏	**der Montag** *(mohn-tahk)*	. . . .	Monday
❏	**der Morgen** *(mor-gen)*	. . . .	morning

m

_____
_____
_____
_____

Study the following patterns carefully.

(eeH) **ich** I	*(koh-muh)* **komme**	=	I *come*
	(gay-uh) **gehe**	=	I *go*
	(lair-nuh) **lerne**	=	I *learn*
	(brow-Huh) **brauche**	=	I *need*
	(huh-buh) **habe**	=	I *have*
	(murk-tuh) **möchte***	=	I *would like*

(air) **er** *(zee)* **sie** she *(es)* **es**	*(kohmt)* **kommt**	=	he, she or it *comes*
	(gate) **geht**	=	he, she or it *goes*
	(lairnt) **lernt**	=	he, she or it *learns*
	(browHt) **braucht**	=	he, she or it *needs*
	(haht) **hat***	=	he, she or it *has*
	(murk-tuh) **möchte***	=	he, she or it *would like*

Note: • With all these verbs, the first thing you do is drop the final "en" from the basic

verb form or stem.

• With "*(eeH)* **ich**," add "**e**" to the basic verb form.

• With "*(air)* **er**," "*(zee)* **sie**," or "**es**," add "**t**."

• *(murk-tuh)* **Möchte** varies, but not too much. It is a very important verb so take a few extra

minutes to learn it

*Some verbs just will not conform to the pattern! But don't worry. Speak slowly **und** clearly,

und you will be perfectly understood whether you say „hat" or „haben." German speakers will

will be delighted you have taken the time to learn their language.

Note: • German has three separate and very different ways of saying "you" whereas in

English we only use one word.

• *(zee)* „**Sie**" will be used throughout this book and will be appropriate for most
you

situations. *(zee)* „**Sie**" refers to both one or more persons in a formal sense.
you

• *(doo)* „**Du**" and its plural form *(ear)* „**ihr**," are forms of address usually reserved for
you (singular)   you (plural)

family members and very close friends.

☐	**der Mund** *(moont)*	mouth		
☐	**das Museum** *(moo-zay-oom)*	museum	**m**	
☐	**die Musik** *(moo-zeek)*	music		
☐	**die Mutter** *(moo-tair)*	mother	**n**	
☐	**nächst** *(nekst)*	next		

Here's your next group of patterns! With „**wir**,"*(vir)* „**Sie**"*(zee)* or „**sie**,"*(zee)* there is no change at all!

we   you   they

(vir) **wir**	*(koh-men)* **kommen**	= we, you, or they *come*	*(brow-Hen)* **brauchen**	= we, you, or they *need*
(zee) **Sie** you	*(gay-en)* **gehen**	= we, you, or they *go*	*(hah-ben)* **haben**	= we, you, or they *have*
(zee) **sie** they	*(lair-nen)* **lernen**	= we, you, or they *learn*	*(murk-ten)* **möchten**	= we, you, or they *would like*

Note: **Sie haben** only **zwei***(tsvy)* changes to remember.

ich*(eeH)* ⟶ is followed by verbs with an "e" on the end . . . . *ex.*   **ich brauch<u>e</u>**

er, sie, es*(air)* ⟶ are followed by verbs with a "t" on the end . . . . *ex.*   **er brauch<u>t</u>**
                                                                       sie brauch<u>t</u>
                                                                       es brauch<u>t</u>

Hier sind sechs*(zeks)* more **Verben.***(vair-ben)*

here   are   six   verbs

(kow-fen) **kaufen** _____
to buy

(voh-nen) **wohnen**   wohnen, wohnen _____
to live, to reside

(shpreh-Hen) **sprechen** _____
to speak

(beh-shtel-len) **bestellen** _____
to order

(bly-ben) **bleiben** _____
to stay, to remain

(hi-sen) **heißen** _____
to be named

At the back of **das Buch,***(booH)* **Sie***(zee)* will find twelve

Seiten*(zy-ten)* of flash cards to help you learn these
pages

neue Wörter.*(noy-uh)* Cut them out; carry them in
new

your briefcase, purse, pocket **oder***(oh-dair)* knapsack;
                                             or

review them whenever **Sie haben***(hah-ben)* a free

moment.

❑	**die Nacht** *(nahHt)*	night	_____
	— **Gute Nacht!** *(goo-tuh)(nahHt)*	good night!	_____
❑	**der Name** *(nah-muh)*	name	_____
❑	**die Nation** *(nah-tsee-ohn)*	nation	_____
❑	**die Nationalität** *(nah-tsee-oh-nahl-ih-tate)*	nationality	

n

Nun, it is your turn to practice what **Sie** *(zee)* have learned. Fill in the following blanks with the correct form of the verb. Each time **Sie** *(zee)* write out the sentence, be sure to say it aloud.

(koh-men)
kommen
to come

Ich _____ aus Amerika. *(ows)* *(ah-mair-ih-kah)*
from

Er
Sie _____ aus Kanada. *(kah-nah-dah)*
Es

Wir _____ aus Holland. *(hohl-lahnt)*

Sie _____ aus England. *(eng-lahnt)*
you

Sie _____ aus Deutschland.
they

(gay-en)
gehen
to go

Ich _____ morgen abend. *(ah-bent)*

Er
Sie _____ ins Restaurant.
Es

Wir _____ mit dem Hund. *(mit)* *(hoont)*
with

Sie _____ heute abend.
you

Sie _____ in die Küche.
they

(hah-ben)
haben
to have

Ich _____ zehn Euro. *(tsayn)*

Er
Sie _____ vierzig Euro. *(fear-tsig)*
Es

Wir _____ dreißig Euro. *(dry-sig)*

Sie _____ zwanzig Euro. *(tsvahn tsig)*
you

Sie _____ hundert Euro. *(hoon-dairt)*
they

(lair-nen)
lernen
to learn

Ich _____ Deutsch. *(doych)*

Er
Sie _____ Japanisch. *(yah-pah-nish)*
Es

Wir _____ Italienisch. *(ee-tah-lee-ay-nish)*

Sie _____ Englisch. *(eng-lish)*
you

Sie _____ Spanisch. *(shpah-nish)*
they

(brow-Hen)
brauchen
to need

Ich _____ ein Zimmer. *(ein)* *(tsih-mair)*

Er
Sie _____ ein Glas Wasser. *(glahs)* *(vah-sair)*
Es glass water

Wir _____ zwei Glas Wein. *(vine)*
wine

Sie _____ eine Tasse Tee. *(tah-suh)* *(tay)*
you cup

Sie _____ vier Tassen Kaffee. *(fear)* *(kah-fay)*
they

(murk-ten)
möchten
would like

Ich _____ ein Glas Wein.

Er
Sie _____ eine Tasse Kakao. *(tah-suh)* *(kah-kow)*
Es cup hot chocolate

Wir _____ drei Glas Weißwein. *(vice-vine)*
white wine

Sie _____ ein Glas Milch. *(milsh)*
you

Sie _____ zwei Glas Bier. *(tsvy)*
they

❏	**natürlich** *(nah-tewr-leeH)*	naturally
❏	**der November** *(noh-vem-bair)*	November
❏	**die Nummer** *(noo-mair)*	number
❏	**der Ofen** *(oh-fen)*	oven
❏	**oft** *(ohft)*	often

n _____
_____
o _____
_____
_____

43

Now take a break, walk around the room, take a deep breath **und** do the next *(zeks)* **sechs** verbs.

(kow-fen)
kaufen
to buy

Ich _____ ein Buch. *(booH)*

Er
Sie _____ einen Salat. *(eye-nen) (zah-laht)*
Es

Wir _____ ein Auto. *(ow-toh)*

Sie _____ eine Uhr. *(eye-nuh) (oor)*
you

Sie _____ sieben Karten. *(zee-ben) (kar-ten)*
they
tickets

(beh-shtel-len)
bestellen
to order

Ich _____ ein Glas Wasser. *(glahs) (vah-sair)*
water

Er
Sie _____ ein Glas Wein. *(vine)*
Es

Wir _____ zwei Tassen Tee. *(tah-sen) (tay)*

Sie _____ eine Tasse Kaffee. *(kah-fay)*
you

Sie _____ drei Tassen Tee. *(dry)*
they

(voh-nen)
wohnen
to live, to reside

Ich _____ in Deutschland. *(doych-lahnt)*

Er
Sie _____ in Amerika. *(ah-mair-ih-kah)*
Es

Wir _____ in einem Hotel. *(eye-nem)*

Sie _____ in Europa. *(oy-roh-pah)*
you

Sie _____ in Japan. *(yah-pahn)*
they

(bly-ben)
bleiben
to stay, to remain

Ich _____ noch fünf Tage. *(nohH) (fewnf) (tah-guh)*
still   days

Er
Sie _____ noch drei Tage. *(nohH) (dry)*
Es

Wir _____ in Deutschland. *(doych-lahnt)*

Sie _____ in Berlin. *(bair-leen)*
you

Sie _____ in Frankfurt. *(frahnk-foort)*
they

(shpreh-Hen)
sprechen
to speak

> Ich spreche Deutsch.

Ich _____ Deutsch. *(doych)*

Er
Sie spricht/ _____ Englisch. *(eng-lish)*
Es

Wir _____ Spanisch. *(shpah-nish)*

Sie _____ Dänisch. *(day-nish)*
you

Sie _____ Japanisch. *(yah-pah-nish)*
they

(hi-sen)
heißen
to be called

> Ich heiße Karla.

Ich _____ Doktor Müller. *(dohk-tor) (mew-lair)*

Er
Sie _____ Zimmermann. *(tsih-mair-mahn)*
Es

Wir _____ Faber. *(fah-bair)*

Sie _____ Seehafer. *(zay-hah-fair)*
you

Sie _____ Familie Nickel. *(fah-mee-lee-uh)*
they

□ **offen** *(ohf-fen)* . . . . open _____
— **Das Restaurant ist offen.**

□ **offiziel** *(oh-fee-tsee-el)* . . . . official **O** _____

□ **der Offizier** *(oh-fee-tseer)* . . . . officer _____

44 □ **der Oktober** *(ohk-toh-bair)* . . . . October _____

Ja, *(yah)* / yes — it is hard to get used to all those new words. Just keep practicing **und** before **Sie** *(zee)* know it, **Sie** will be using them naturally. **Nun** *(noon)* is a perfect time to turn to the back of this **Buch**, clip out your verb flash cards **und** start flashing. Don't skip over your free **Wörter** either. Check them off in the box provided as **Sie lernen** *(lair-nen)* / learn each one. See if **Sie** can fill in the blanks below. **Die richtigen Antworten** *(ahnt-vor-ten)* **sind** at the bottom of the **Seite** *(zy-tuh)* / page.

1. _____
(I speak German.)

2. _____
(We learn German.)

3. _____
(She needs 10 Euro.)

4. _____
(He comes from Canada.)

5. _____
(They live in Germany.)

6. _____
(You buy a book.)

In the following Steps, **Sie** *(zee)* will be introduced to more verbs **und Sie** should drill them in exactly the same way as **Sie** did in this section. Look up **die** *(dee)* **neuen** *(noy-en)* **Wörter** / new in your **Wörterbuch** *(vur-tair-booH)* / dictionary **und** make up your own sentences. Try out your **neue** *(noy-uh)* **Wörter** for that's how you make them yours to use on your holiday. Remember, the more **Sie** practice **jetzt** *(yets-t)* / now, the more enjoyable your trip will be. **Viel** *(feel)* / good **Glück!** *(glewk)* / luck

(zee) Sie know how to tell die *(tah-guh)* Tage of the *(voh-Huh)* Woche und die *(moh-nah-tuh)* Monate of the *(yar)* Jahr, so let's learn to tell

days   week   months   year

time. Punctuality in Deutschland ist *(zair)* sehr *(veeH-teeg)* wichtig, plus Sie need to be able to tell time in order

very   important

to make *(rez-air-veer-oong-en)* Reservierungen, und to catch *(tsue-guh)* Züge und *(boo-suh)* Busse. Hier sind the basics.

reservations   trains   here   are

What time is it?	=	*(vee-feel)* *(oor)* *(ist)* *(es)* **Wieviel Uhr ist es?**
noon	=	*(mit-tahk)* **Mittag**
midnight	=	*(mit-tair-nahHt)* **Mitternacht**
half	=	*(hahlp)* **halb**
before/to	=	*(for)* **vor**
after	=	*(nahH)* **nach**
a quarter	=	*(ein)* *(fear-tel)* **ein Viertel**
a quarter to	=	*(for)* **Viertel vor**
a quarter after	=	*(fear-tel)* *(nahH)* **Viertel nach**

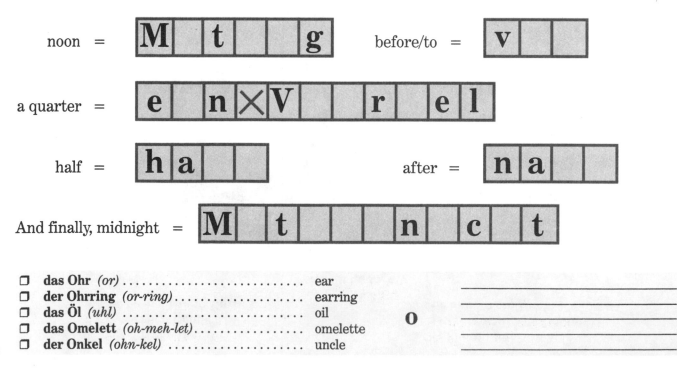

Nun quiz yourself. Fill in the missing letters below.

noon = | M | | t | | g | before/to = | v | | |

a quarter = | e | | n | ╳ | V | | r | | e | l |

half = | h | a | | after = | n | a | |

And finally, midnight = | M | | t | | | n | | c | | t |

☐	**das Ohr** *(or)*	ear		_____
☐	**der Ohrring** *(or-ring)*	earring		_____
☐	**das Öl** *(uhl)*	oil	**o**	_____
☐	**das Omelett** *(oh-meh-let)*	omelette		_____
☐	**der Onkel** *(ohn-kel)*	uncle		_____

Nun, *(vee)* **wie** *(zint)* **sind** these **Wörter** used? Study the examples below.   When **Sie** think it through,
how

it really is not too difficult. Just notice that the pattern changes after the halfway mark. You'll

see that the phrase "o'clock" is not used in German.

Es ist *(fewnf)* **fünf Uhr.**
it   five o'clock

`5:00`

Es ist fünf Uhr.

Es ist *(tsayn)* **zehn** *(nahH)* **nach fünf.**

`5:10`

_____

Es ist *(fear-tel)* **Viertel nach fünf.**

`5:15`

_____

Es ist *(tsvahn-tsig)* **zwanzig nach fünf.**

`5:20`

_____

Es ist *(hahlp)* **halb** *(zeks)* **sechs.**
half   six

`5:30`

_____

Es ist zwanzig *(for)* **vor sechs.**

`5:40`

_____

Es ist Viertel vor sechs.

`5:45`

_____

Es ist *(tsayn)* **zehn vor sechs.**

`5:50`

_____

Es ist sechs *(oor)* **Uhr.**

`6:00`

_____

See how *(veeH-teeg)* **wichtig** it is to learn **die Nummern?** Answer the following *(frah-gen)* **Fragen** based on the
questions

Uhren below. *(vee-feel)* **Wieviel Uhr ist es?**
clocks

1. `8:00` _____

2. `7:15` _____

3. `4:30` _____

4. `9:20` _____

ANTWORTEN

4. **Es ist zwanzig nach neun.**

3. **Es ist halb fünf.**

2. **Es ist Viertel nach sieben.**

1. **Es ist acht Uhr.**

When **Sie** answer a „ **Wann?** " _(vahn)_ question, say „ **um** " _(oom)_ before **Sie** give the time.

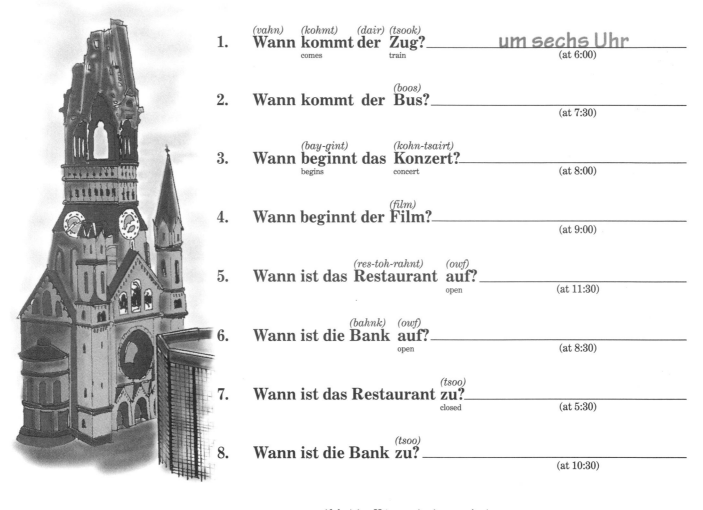

1. **Wann** _(vahn)_ **kommt** _(kohmt)_ **der** _(dair)_ **Zug?** _(tsook)_ ___um sechs Uhr___
   comes train _(at 6:00)_

2. **Wann kommt der Bus?** _(boos)_ _____
   _(at 7:30)_

3. **Wann beginnt** _(bay-gint)_ **das Konzert?** _(kohn-tsairt)_ _____
   begins concert _(at 8:00)_

4. **Wann beginnt der Film?** _(film)_ _____
   _(at 9:00)_

5. **Wann ist das Restaurant** _(res-toh-rahnt)_ **auf?** _(owf)_ _____
   open _(at 11:30)_

6. **Wann ist die Bank** _(bahnk)_ **auf?** _(owf)_ _____
   open _(at 8:30)_

7. **Wann ist das Restaurant zu?** _(tsoo)_ _____
   closed _(at 5:30)_

8. **Wann ist die Bank zu?** _(tsoo)_ _____
   _(at 10:30)_

Hier ist a quick quiz. Fill in the blanks **mit** _(with)_ **den** _(dehn)_ **richtigen** _(reeH-tee-gen)_ **Nummern.** _(noo-mairn)_

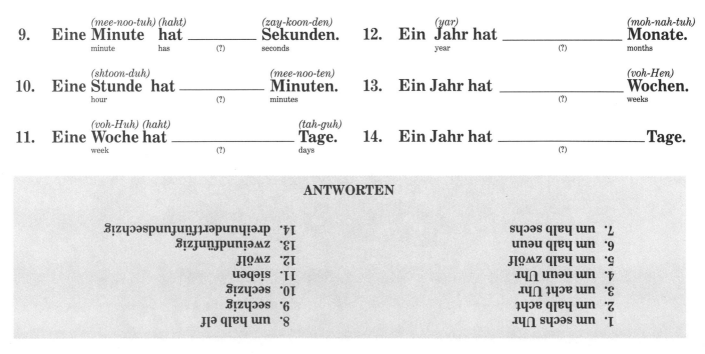

9. **Eine Minute** _(mee-noo-tuh)_ **hat** _(haht)_ _____ **Sekunden.** _(zay-koon-den)_
   minute has _(?)_ seconds

10. **Eine Stunde** _(shtoon-duh)_ **hat** _____ **Minuten.** _(mee-noo-ten)_
    hour _(?)_ minutes

11. **Eine Woche hat** _(voh-Huh)(haht)_ _____ **Tage.** _(tah-guh)_
    week _(?)_ days

12. **Ein Jahr hat** _(yar)_ _____ **Monate.** _(moh-nah-tuh)_
    year _(?)_ months

13. **Ein Jahr hat** _____ **Wochen.** _(voh-Hen)_
    _(?)_ weeks

14. **Ein Jahr hat** _____ **Tage.**
    _(?)_

ANTWORTEN

14. dreihundertfünfundsechzig
13. zweiundfünfzig
12. zwölf
11. sieben
10. sechzig
9. sechzig
8. **um halb elf**

7. **um halb sechs**
6. **um halb neun**
5. **um halb zwölf**
4. **um neun Uhr**
3. **um acht Uhr**
2. **um halb acht**
1. **um sechs Uhr**

Do **Sie** *(zee)* remember your greetings from earlier? It is a good time to review them as they will

always be **sehr** *(zair)* **wichtig.** *(veeH-teeg)*
very   important

Um acht Uhr *(oom)* **morgens** *(mor-gens)* **sagt** *(zahkt)* **man,** *(mahn)* „**Guten** *(goo-ten)* **Morgen, Frau** *(frow)* **Bernhard!"** *(bairn-hart)*
at   in the morning   says   one   good   morning   Mrs.

Was *(vahs)* **sagt man?** *(zahkt)* _Guten Morgen, Frau Bernhard!_
what does one say

Um ein Uhr *(ein)* **nachmittags** *(nahH-mit-tahgs)* **sagt man,** *(zahkt)* „**Guten Tag,** *(tahk)* **Herr** *(hair)* **Richter!"** *(reeH-tair)*
one   in the afternoon   Mr.

Was sagt man? *(vahs) (zahkt) (mahn)* _____

Um acht Uhr abends *(ah-bents)* **sagt man,** *(zahkt)* „**Guten Abend,** *(ah-bent)* **Fräulein** *(froy-line)* **Seehafer."** *(zay-hah-fair)*
in the evening   Miss

Was sagt man? *(vahs)* _____

Um zehn Uhr abends sagt man, „**Gute** *(goo-tuh)* **Nacht."** *(nahHt)*
ten

Was sagt man? *(mahn)* _____
one

Sie have probably already noticed that plurals are formed in a variety of ways.

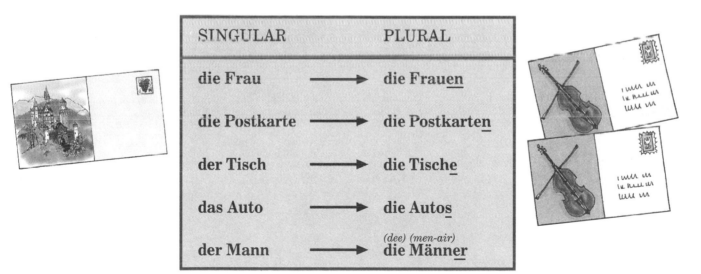

SINGULAR		PLURAL
die Frau	⟶	die Frau**en**
die Postkarte	⟶	die Postkarte**n**
der Tisch	⟶	die Tisch**e**
das Auto	⟶	die Auto**s**
der Mann	⟶	die Män**ner** *(dee) (men-air)*

Know that **deutsche Wörter** change their endings in the plural so always listen for the core of

the word.

- ❏ **die Oper** *(oh-pair)* . . . . opera _____
  — **Ich gehe in die Oper.**
- ❏ **das Opernhaus** *(oh-pairn-house)* . . . . opera house **O** _____
  — **Das Opernhaus ist sehr alt.**
- ❏ **die Ordnung** *(ord-noong)* . . . . order _____

Hier sind zwei neue *(noy-uh)* **Verben** *(fewr)* **für** Step 13.

(ess-en)
essen _____
to eat

(trink-en)
trinken _____
to drink

(ess-en)
essen
to eat

(trink-en)
trinken
to drink

Ich _____	*(vee-nair) (shnit-tsel)* **Wiener Schnitzel.**	
Er **Sie** _ißt/_____ **Es**	*(fish)* **Fisch.**	
Wir _____	*(feel)* **viel.** a lot	
Sie _____ you	**ein Beefsteak.**	
Sie _____	*(lahm)* **Lamm.** lamb	

Ich _____	*(milsh)* **Milch.**	
Er **Sie** _trinkt/_____ **Es**	*(neeH-ts)* **nichts.** nothing	
Wir _____	*(mih-nair-ahl-vah-sair)* **Mineralwasser.**	
Sie _____	*(toh-mah-ten-zahft)* **Tomatensaft.** tomato juice	
Sie _____ they	*(kah-kow)* **Kakao.** hot chocolate	

Remember that „a" sounds like "ah." Practice **Land,** *(lahnt)* **schlafen,** *(shlah-fen)* **baden,** *(bah-den)* **danke,** *(dahn-kuh)* **was, wann** and **Bank.** *(bahnk)* Also „au" is pronounced "ow" as in "Wow!" Practice **Frau,** **auf,** *(owf)* **kaufen,** *(kow-fen)* **August** *(ow-goost)* and **aus.** *(ows)*

❐ **das Orchester** *(or-kes-tair)* . . . . orchestra   _____
  — **Das Orchester in Berlin ist sehr gut.**   _____
❐ **die Organisation** *(or-gahn-ih-zah-tsee-ohn)* . organization   **o** _____
❐ **die Orgel** *(or-gel)* . . . . organ   _____
  — **Die Orgel ist nicht neu.**   _____

Sie haben *(hah-ben)* learned a lot of material in the last few steps **und** that means it is time to quiz yourself. Don't panic, this is just for you **und** no one else needs to know how **Sie** did. Remember, this is a chance to review, find out what **Sie** remember **und** what **Sie** need to spend more time on. After **Sie** have finished, check your **Antworten** in the glossary at the back of this book. Circle the correct answers.

der Kaffee	tea	coffee
ja	yes	no
die Tante	aunt	uncle
oder	and	or
lernen	to drink	to learn
die Nacht	morning	night
Freitag	Friday	Tuesday
sprechen	to live	to speak
der Winter	summer	winter
das Geld	money	page
zehn	nine	ten
viel	a lot	bread

die Familie	seven	family
die Kinder	children	grandfather
die Milch	butter	(milk)
das Salz	pepper	salt
über	under	over
der Mann	man	doctor
der Juni	June	July
die Küche	kitchen	religions
ich habe	I want	I have
kaufen	to order	to buy
gestern	yesterday	tomorrow
gut	good	yellow

(vee) (gate) (ee-nen)
Wie geht es Ihnen?   What time is it?   How are you?   Well, how are you after this quiz?

❐ **der Ozean** *(oh-tsay-ahn)* . . . . ocean
   — **Der Ozean ist blau und grün.**
❐ **ein Paar** *(ein)(par)* . . . . a pair, a couple
❐ **packen** *(pah-ken)* . . . . to pack
❐ **das Paket** *(pah-kate)* . . . . package

o _____
_____
p _____
_____

If **Sie** are looking at **eine** (lahnt-kar-tuh) **Landkarte und Sie** see the following **Wörter,** it should not be too difficult to figure out what they mean. Take an educated guess.

(nort-ah-mair-ih-kah) **das Nordamerika**

(zewt-ah-mair-ih-kah) **das Südamerika**

(ohst-kews-tuh) **die Ostküste**

(vest-kews-tuh) **die Westküste**

(nort-pohl) **der Nordpol**

(zewt-pohl) **der Südpol**

(nort-zay) **die Nordsee**

(zewt-ah-frih-kah) **das Südafrika**

Die deutschen Wörter (fewr) **für** "north," "south," "east," **und** "west" are easy to recognize due to their similarity to **Englisch.** These **Wörter sind** (zair) **sehr** (veeH-teeg) **wichtig.** Learn them (yets-t) **jetzt!**

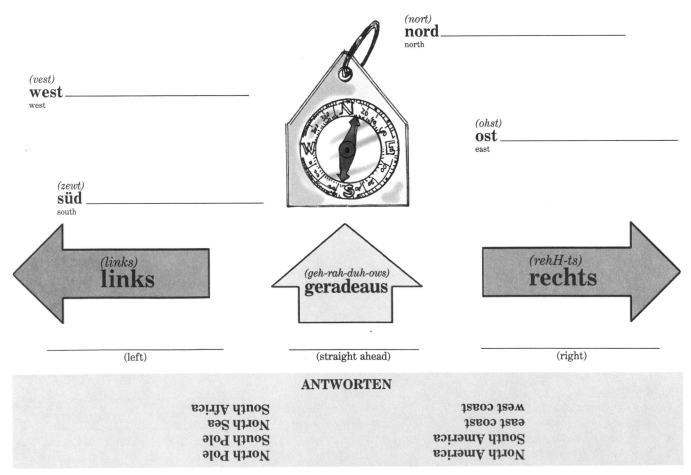

(nort) **nord** _____
north

(vest) **west** _____
west

(ohst) **ost** _____
east

(zewt) **süd** _____
south

(links) **links**

(geh-rah-duh-ows) **geradeaus**

(rehH-ts) **rechts**

_____ (left)

_____ (straight ahead)

_____ (right)

These **Wörter** can go a long way. Say them aloud each time you write them in the blanks below.

(bit-tuh)
bitte _____
please

(dahn-kuh)
danke _____
thank you

(ent-shool-dee-goong)   *(fair-tsy-oong)*
Entschuldigung/ Verzeihung _____
excuse me

(bit-tuh)
bitte _____
you're welcome

          (tsvy) *(zair)* *(too-pish-uh)* *(kohn-vair-zah-tsee-oh-nen)* *(fewr)*
Hier sind zwei sehr typische Konversationen für someone who is trying to find something.
                        typical   conversations

Write them out in the blanks below.

Karl:
(ent-shool-dee-goong)   *(rit-tair)*
Entschuldigung. Wo ist das Hotel Ritter?
                                        knight

___**Entschuldigung. Wo ist das Hotel Ritter?**___

Heinz:
(gay-en)   *(shtrah-sen)* *(vy-tair)* *(dahn)*
Gehen Sie zwei Straßen weiter, dann links.
go   streets   further   then

_____

(owf)   *(rehH-ten)* *(zy-tuh)*
Das Hotel Ritter ist auf der rechten Seite.
              on   right   side

_____

Thomas:
(ent-shool-dee-goong)   *(moo-zay-oom)*
Entschuldigung. Wo ist das Deutsche Museum?

_____

Helga:
(gay-en)   *(geh-rah-duh-ows)*   *(oon-geh-fair)*   *(vy-tair)*
Gehen Sie geradeaus. Ungefähr hundert Meter weiter
                 straight ahead   approximately

_____

(owf)   *(zy-tuh)*
auf der linken Seite ist das Deutsche Museum.
on

_____

❑ **das Papier** *(pah-peer)*	paper		_____
❑ **der Park** *(park)*	park		_____
❑ **der Passagier** *(pah-sah-zheer)*	passenger	**p**	_____
❑ **der Paß** *(pahs)*	passport		_____
❑ **die Paßkontrolle** *(pahs-kohn-trohl-luh)*	passport control, check		_____

Are **Sie** *(zee)* lost? There is no need to be lost if **Sie haben** *(hah-ben)* learned the basic direction **Wörter.** Do not

have
try to memorize these **Konversationen** because **Sie** will never be looking for precisely these

places. One day, **Sie** might need to ask directions to „**das Goethe Museum**" *(guh-tuh)* or „**das Hotel**

Europa." *(oy-roh-pah)* Learn the key direction **Wörter und** be sure **Sie** can find your destination. **Sie** may

want to buy a guidebook to start planning which places **Sie** would like to visit. Practice asking

directions to these special places. What if the person responding to your **Frage** *(frah-guh)* answers too

question
quickly for **Sie** to understand the entire reply? Practice saying,

---

Entschuldigung. Ich verstehe nicht. Wiederholen Sie das bitte.
(fair-shtay-uh) (neeHt)   *(vee-dair-hoh-len)*
do not understand   repeat   that

Nun, say it again **und** then write it out below.

_____

(Excuse me. I do not understand. Please repeat that.)

Ja, es ist schwer *(yah) (shvair)* at first but don't give up! When the directions are repeated, **Sie** will be able to

yes   difficult
understand if **Sie haben** learned the key **Wörter.** Let's review by writing them in the blanks below.

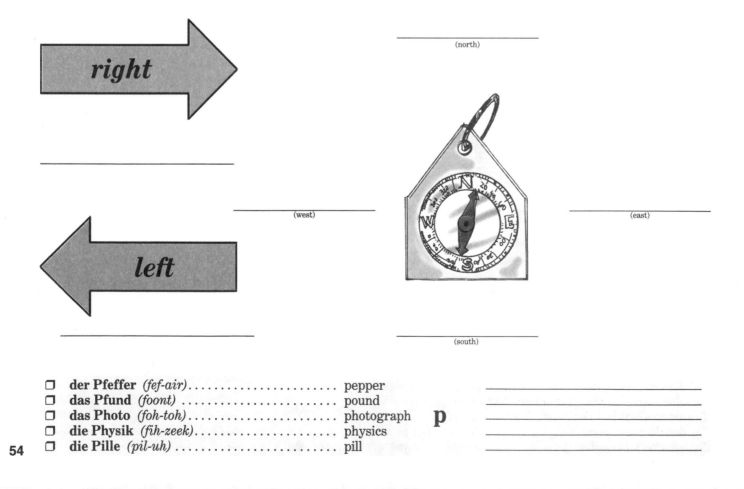

right

left

_____
(north)

_____
(west)

_____
(east)

_____
(south)

❐ **der Pfeffer** *(fef-air)*	pepper	_____
❐ **das Pfund** *(foont)*	pound	_____
❐ **das Photo** *(foh-toh)*	photograph	_____
❐ **die Physik** *(fih-zeek)*	physics	_____
❐ **die Pille** *(pil-uh)*	pill	_____

p

Hier sind vier *(fear)* **neue Verben.**

(zah-gen)
sagen _____
to say

(fair-kow-fen)
verkaufen _____
to sell

(fair-shtay-en)
verstehen _____
to understand

(vee-dair-hoh-len)
wiederholen _____
to repeat

As always, say each sentence out loud. Say each **und** every *(vort)* **Wort** carefully, pronouncing each

German sound as well as **Sie** can.

(zah-gen)
sagen
to say

> Guten Tag!

Ich _____ „Guten Tag."

Er
Sie _____ „nein." *(nine)*
Es   no

Wir _____ „Gute Nacht."

Sie _____ „ ja."
you

Sie _____ nichts. *(neeH-ts)*
                       nothing

(fair-shtay-en)
verstehen
to understand

> Ich verstehe Deutsch.

Ich _____ Englisch.

Er
Sie versteht/ _____ Italienisch. *(ee-tah-lee-ay-nish)*
Es

Wir _____ Deutsch.

Sie _____ Russisch. *(roo-sish)*
                       Russian
Sie _____ Dänisch. *(day-nish)*
they   Danish

(fair-kow-fen)
verkaufen
to sell

Ich _____ Blumen. *(bloo-men)*

Er
Sie _____ nichts. *(neeH-ts)*
Es   nothing

Wir _____ Postkarten.

Sie _____ Wein und Bier. *(vine)*
you

Sie _____ Briefmarken. *(breef-mar-ken)*
                       stamps

(vee-dair-hoh-len)
wiederholen
to repeat

> Bitte? Bitte? Bitte?

Ich _____ das Wort.

Er
Sie _____ die Frage. *(frah-guh)*
Es   question

Wir _____ die Namen.
                         names

Sie _____ die Antworten.
                         answers
Sie _____ die Adresse. *(ah-dres-suh)*
they

☐ **das Polen** *(poh-len)* .... Poland
  — **wo sie Polnisch sprechen** *(pohl-nish)*
☐ **die Police** *(poh-lee-suh)* .... policy (insurance)
☐ **die Polizei** *(poh-lih-tsy)* .... police
☐ **die Politik** *(poh-lih-teek)* .... politics

p

_____

_____

_____

_____

55

15

(oh-ben)   *(oon-ten)*
Oben – Unten
above/upstairs   below/downstairs

(noon) *(lair-nen)* *(vir)* *(mair)*
Nun lernen wir mehr Wörter. Hier ist ein Haus in Deutschland. Gehen Sie in your
    more   *(doych-lahnt)*   *(gay-en)*
                  house

(shlahf-tsih-mair)   *(tsih-mair)*   *(nah-men)*
Schlafzimmer und look around **das Zimmer.** Let's learn **die Namen** of the **Dinge in dem**
bedroom   room   names

(tsih-mair)
Zimmer, just like **wir** learned the various parts of the **Haus.**

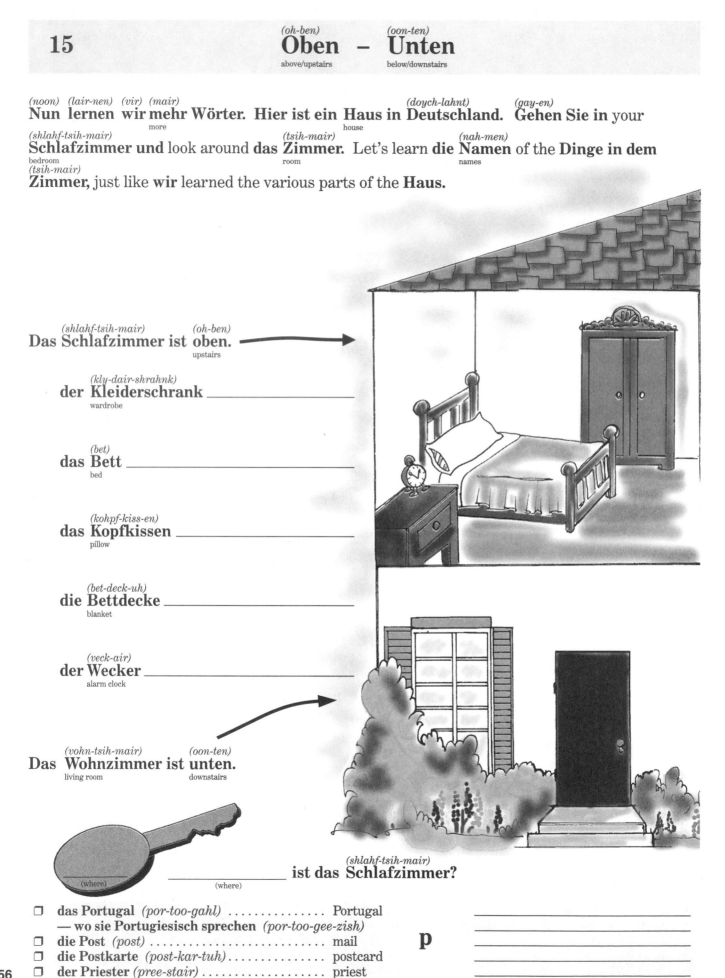

(shlahf-tsih-mair)   *(oh-ben)*
Das Schlafzimmer ist oben.
                    upstairs

(kly-dair-shrahnk)
der Kleiderschrank _____
wardrobe

(bet)
das Bett _____
bed

(kohpf-kiss-en)
das Kopfkissen _____
pillow

(bet-deck-uh)
die Bettdecke _____
blanket

(veck-air)
der Wecker _____
alarm clock

(vohn-tsih-mair)   *(oon-ten)*
Das Wohnzimmer ist unten.
living room   downstairs

(shlahf-tsih-mair)
_____ **ist das Schlafzimmer?**
(where)   (where)

❑ **das Portugal** *(por-too-gahl)* .... Portugal   _____
— **wo sie Portugiesisch sprechen** *(por-too-gee-zish)*   _____
❑ **die Post** *(post)* .... mail   **p**   _____
❑ **die Postkarte** *(post-kar-tuh)* .... postcard   _____
56 ❑ **der Priester** *(pree-stair)* .... priest   _____

Jetzt, *(yets-t)* remove the next **fünf** *(fewnf)* stickers **und** label these things **in** your **Schlafzimmer.** *(shlahf-tsih-mair)* Let's move
now

into **das Badezimmer und** *(bah-duh-tsih-mair)* do the same thing. Remember, **das Badezimmer** *(bah-duh-tsih-mair)* means a room to
bathroom

bathe in. If **Sie sind in einem Restaurant und Sie** *(zee) (zint)* need to use the lavatory, **Sie** want to ask for

die Toilette und *(toy-let-tuh)* *not* for **das Badezimmer.** Restrooms may be marked with pictures

oder simply the letters **D** oder **H.** Don't confuse them!

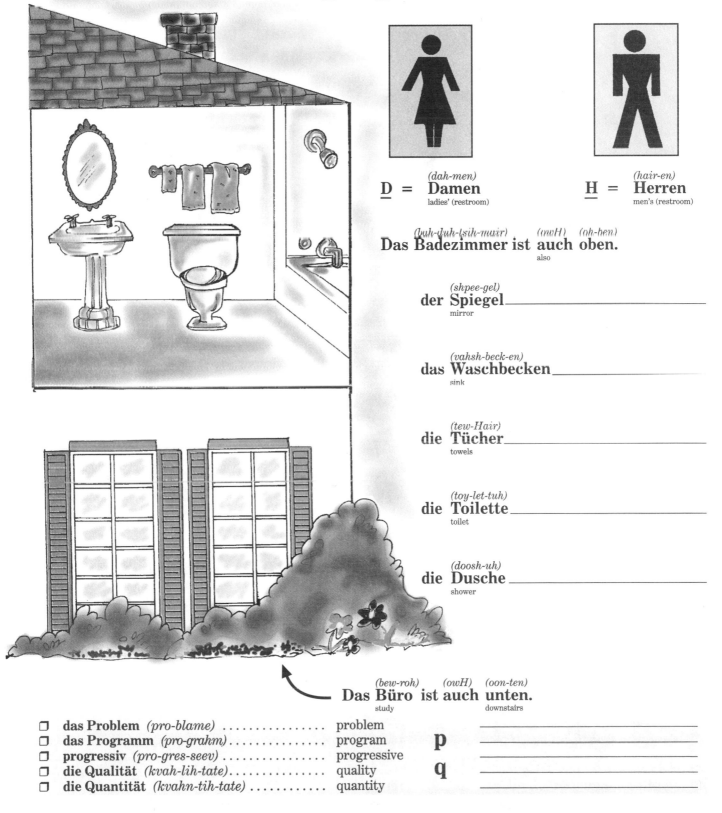

D = **Damen** *(dah-men)*
ladies' (restroom)

H = **Herren** *(hair-en)*
men's (restroom)

Das Badezimmer ist auch oben. *(bah-duh-tsih-mair) (owH) (oh-hen)*
also

der **Spiegel** *(shpee-gel)* _____
mirror

das **Waschbecken** *(vahsh-beck-en)* _____
sink

die **Tücher** *(tew-Hair)* _____
towels

die **Toilette** *(toy-let-tuh)* _____
toilet

die **Dusche** *(doosh-uh)* _____
shower

Das Büro ist auch unten. *(bew-roh) (owH) (oon-ten)*
study   downstairs

❏	**das Problem** *(pro-blame)*	problem	
❏	**das Programm** *(pro-grahm)*	program	**p** _____
❏	**progressiv** *(pro-gres-seev)*	progressive	_____
❏	**die Qualität** *(kvah-lih-tate)*	quality	**q** _____
❏	**die Quantität** *(kvahn-tih-tate)*	quantity	_____

Do not forget to remove the next group of stickers **und** label these things in your **Haus.** Okay, it is time to review. Here's a quick quiz to see what you remember.

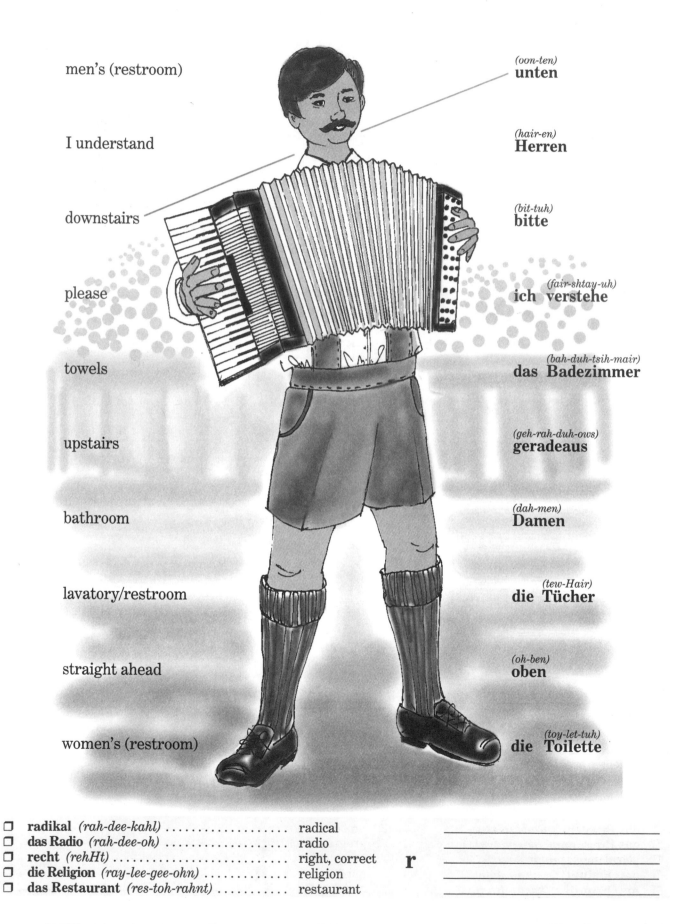

men's (restroom)   *(oon-ten)*
                                    unten

I understand   *(hair-en)*
                                    Herren

downstairs   *(bit-tuh)*
                                    bitte

please   *(fair-shtay-uh)*
                                    ich verstehe

towels   *(bah-duh-tsih-mair)*
                                    das Badezimmer

upstairs   *(geh-rah-duh-ows)*
                                    geradeaus

bathroom   *(dah-men)*
                                    Damen

lavatory/restroom   *(tew-Hair)*
                                    die Tücher

straight ahead   *(oh-ben)*
                                    oben

women's (restroom)   *(toy-let-tuh)*
                                    die Toilette

☐ **radikal** *(rah-dee-kahl)* . . . . radical
☐ **das Radio** *(rah-dee-oh)* . . . . radio
☐ **recht** *(rehHt)* . . . . right, correct   **r**
☐ **die Religion** *(ray-lee-gee-ohn)* . . . . religion
☐ **das Restaurant** *(res-toh-rahnt)* . . . . restaurant

Next stop — **das Büro,** *(bew-roh)* office, specifically **der Tisch** *(tish)* table **oder der Schreibtisch** *(shripe-tish)* desk **in dem Büro.** *(bew-roh)* **Was ist auf** *(vahs)* what *(owf)* on **dem Tisch?** *(dehm)* Let's identify **die Dinge** things which one normally finds **in dem Büro** *(bew-roh)* **oder** strewn about **das Haus.**

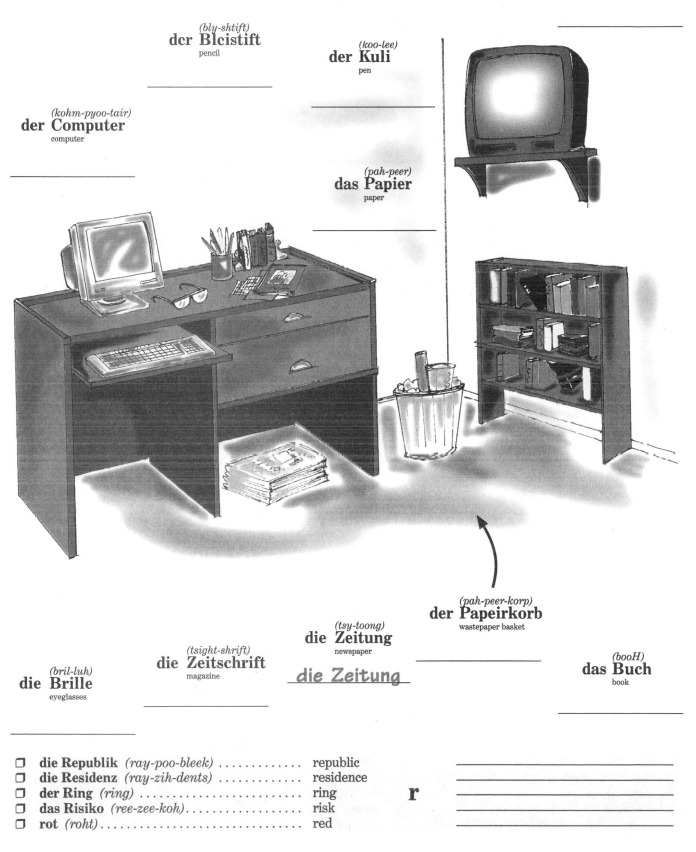

der Fernseher *(fairn-zay-air)* television

_____

dcr Blcistift *(bly-shtift)* pencil

_____

der Kuli *(koo-lee)* pen

_____

der Computer *(kohm-pyoo-tair)* computer

_____

das Papier *(pah-peer)* paper

_____

der Papeirkorb *(pah-peer-korp)* wastepaper basket

_____

die Brille *(bril-luh)* eyeglasses

_____

die Zeitschrift *(tsight-shrift)* magazine

_____

die Zeitung *(tsy-toong)* newspaper

die Zeitung

das Buch *(booH)* book

_____

r

_____
_____
_____
_____
_____

Don't forget these essentials!

der Brief *(breef)*
letter

die Briefmarke *(breef-mar-kuh)*
stamp

die Postkarte *(post-kar-tuh)*
postcard

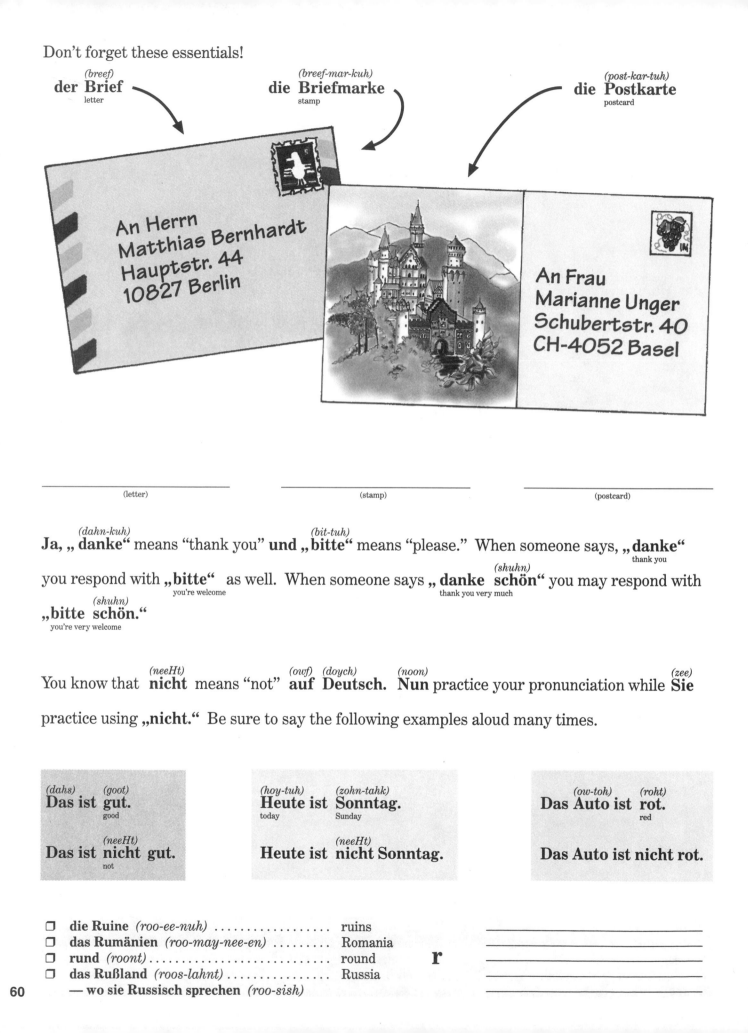

An Herrn
Matthias Bernhardt
Hauptstr. 44
10827 Berlin

An Frau
Marianne Unger
Schubertstr. 40
CH-4052 Basel

_____   _____   _____
(letter)   (stamp)   (postcard)

Ja, „ **danke** " *(dahn-kuh)* means "thank you" **und** „ **bitte** " *(bit-tuh)* means "please." When someone says, „ **danke** " thank you you respond with „ **bitte** " you're welcome as well. When someone says „ **danke schön** " *(shuhn)* thank you very much you may respond with „ **bitte schön.** " *(shuhn)* you're very welcome

You know that **nicht** *(neeHt)* means "not" **auf Deutsch.** *(owf) (doych)* **Nun** *(noon)* practice your pronunciation while **Sie** *(zee)* practice using „ **nicht.** " Be sure to say the following examples aloud many times.

Das ist gut. *(dahs) (goot)*
good

Das ist nicht gut. *(neeHt)*
not

Heute ist Sonntag. *(hoy-tuh) (zohn-tahk)*
today   Sunday

Heute ist nicht Sonntag. *(neeHt)*

Das Auto ist rot. *(ow-toh) (roht)*
red

Das Auto ist nicht rot.

❑ **die Ruine** *(roo-ee-nuh)* . . . . ruins   _____
❑ **das Rumänien** *(roo-may-nee-en)* . . . . Romania   _____
❑ **rund** *(roont)* . . . . round   **r**   _____
❑ **das Rußland** *(roos-lahnt)* . . . . Russia   _____
    — wo sie Russisch sprechen *(roo-sish)*   _____

60

Simple, isn't it? **Nun,** *(noon)* after you fill in the blanks below, go back a second time and negate all these sentences by adding **„nicht."** Don't get discouraged! Just look at how much **Sie** have already learned **und** think ahead to wonderful food, **das Oktoberfest** *(ohk-toh-bair-fest)* **und** new adventures.

(zay-en)
sehen _____
to see

(zen-den)
senden _____
to send

(shlah-fen)
schlafen _____
to sleep

(fin-den)
finden _____
to find

(zay-en)
sehen
to see

Ich _____ das Museum. *(moo-zay-oom)*

Er
Sie sieht/ _____ die Stadt. *(shtaht)* city
Es

Wir _____ die Alpen. *(ahl-pen)* Alps

Sie _____ das Schloß. *(shlohs)* castle
you

Sie _____ die Kirche.

(zen-den)
senden
to send

Ich _____ den Brief. *(breef)*

Er
Sie sendet/ _____ die Postkarte.
Es

Wir _____ das Buch. *(booH)*

Sie _____ drei Postkarten.

Sie _____ vier Briefe.
they

(shlah-fen)
schlafen
to sleep

Ich _____ im Schlafzimmer. *(shlahf-tsih-mair)*

Er
Sie schläft/ _____ im Hotel.
Es

Wir _____ im Hause. *(how-zuh)*

Sie _____ mit Bettdecken. *(bet-deck-en)* blankets

Sie _____ ohne Bettdecken. *(oh-nuh)* without
they

(fin-den)
finden
to find

Ich _____ das Restaurant.

Er
Sie findet/ _____ das Hotel.
Es

Wir _____ die Brille.

Sie _____ das Museum. *(moo-zay-oom)*
you

Sie _____ das Rathaus. *(raht house)* city hall

❑ **der Salat** *(zah-laht)* .... salad
❑ **das Salz** *(zahlts)* .... salt
❑ **sauer** *(zow-air)* .... sour (vs. sweet = **süß**)
❑ **scharf** *(sharf)* .... sharp (spicy)
❑ **der Scheck** *(sheck)* .... check

S
_____
_____
_____
_____

Before **Sie** proceed **mit** the next step, **bitte** identify all the items *(oon-ten)* **unten**.

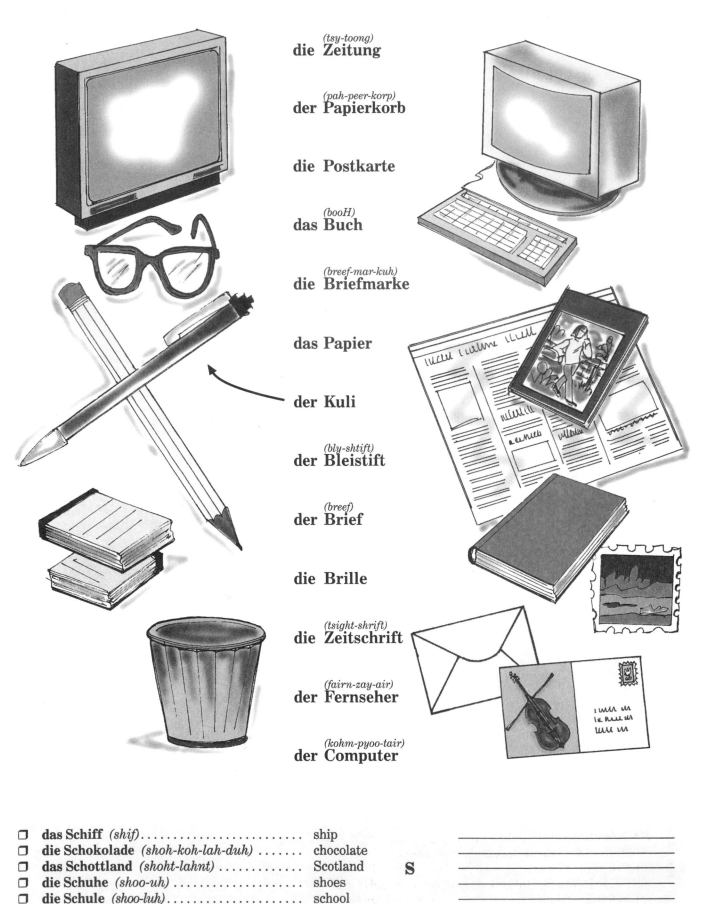

die **Zeitung** *(tsy-toong)*

der **Papierkorb** *(pah-peer-korp)*

die **Postkarte**

das **Buch** *(booH)*

die **Briefmarke** *(breef-mar-kuh)*

das **Papier**

der **Kuli**

der **Bleistift** *(bly-shtift)*

der **Brief** *(breef)*

die **Brille**

die **Zeitschrift** *(tsight-shrift)*

der **Fernseher** *(fairn-zay-air)*

der **Computer** *(kohm-pyoo-tair)*

S

(zee) **Sie** know **nun** *(noon)* how to count, how to ask **Fragen** *(frah-gen)*, how to use **Verben mit** the "plug-in" formula **und** how to describe something, be it the location of a **Hotel oder die Farbe** *(far-buh)* of a **Haus**. Let's take the basics that **Sie haben** learned **und** expand them in special areas that will be most helpful in your travels. What does everyone do on a holiday? Send **Postkarten** of course. Let's learn exactly how **das deutsche Postamt** *(post-ahmt)* works.

post office

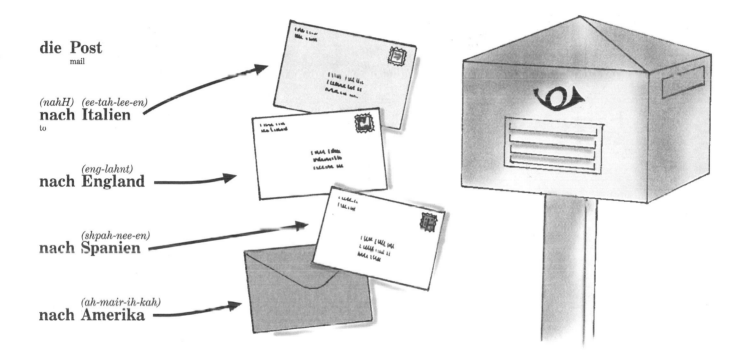

die Post

mail

nach Italien *(nahH)* *(ee-tah-lee-en)*

to

nach England *(eng-lahnt)*

nach Spanien *(shpah-nee-en)*

nach Amerika *(ah-mair-ih-kah)*

Das deutsche Postamt ist *(post-ahmt)* where **Sie** buy **Briefmarken und** send **Briefe und Postkarten**. **Sie** can send **Telegramme** *(tay-lay-grahm-uh)* or make **ein Ferngespräch von dem Postamt** *(fairn-geh-shprayH)*. In large cities, **das Postamt hat ein Schalter** *(haht)* *(shahl-tair)* which is **auf abends und am Samstag**.

post office   telegrams   long-distance call   counter   open   evenings

□ **das Schweden** *(shvay-den)* .... Sweden
    — **wo sie Schwedisch sprechen** *(shvay-dish)*
□ **die Schweiz** *(shvites)* .... Switzerland   **S**
    — **wo sie Deutsch, Italienisch und Französisch sprechen**
□ **schwimmen** *(shvim-en)* .... to swim

_____
_____
_____
_____

Hier sind the necessary **Wörter für das** *(post-ahmt)* **Postamt.** Practice them aloud **und** write them in the
post office

blanks.

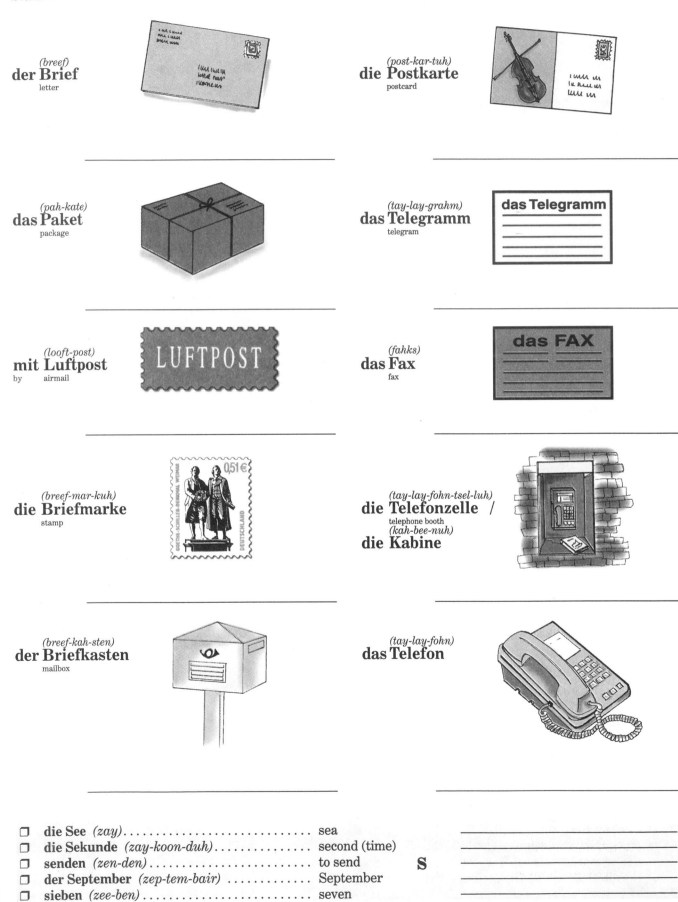

(breef)
der Brief
letter

(post-kar-tuh)
die Postkarte
postcard

(pah-kate)
das Paket
package

(tay-lay-grahm)
das Telegramm
telegram

(looft-post)
mit Luftpost
by   airmail

(fahks)
das Fax
fax

(breef-mar-kuh)
die Briefmarke
stamp

(tay-lay-fohn-tsel-luh)
die Telefonzelle /
telephone booth
(kah-bee-nuh)
die Kabine

(breef-kah-sten)
der Briefkasten
mailbox

(tay-lay-fohn)
das Telefon

☐ **die See** *(zay)* . . . . sea
☐ **die Sekunde** *(zay-koon-duh)* . . . . second (time)
☐ **senden** *(zen-den)* . . . . to send   **S**
☐ **der September** *(zep-tem-bair)* . . . . September
64 ☐ **sieben** *(zee-ben)* . . . . seven

Next step — **Sie** ask **Fragen** *(frah-gen)* like those **unten,** depending on **was Sie möchten.** Repeat these

would like

sentences aloud many times.

Wo *(voh)* **kaufe** *(kow-fuh)* **ich Briefmarken?**_____
do I buy

Wo kaufe ich eine Postkarte?_____

Wo **mache** *(mah-Huh)* **ich einen Telefonanruf?** *(tay-lay-fohn-ahn-roof)* _____
do I make   telephone call

Wo ist **der** *(dair)* **Briefkasten?** *(breef-kah-sten)* _____

Wo ist die **Telefonzelle?** *(tay-lay-fohn-tsel-luh)* _____

Wo **sende** *(zen-duh)* **ich ein Paket?** *(pah-kate)* _____
do I send

Wo **gibt** *(gipt)* **es eine Telefonzelle?** *(tay-lay-fohn-tsel-luh)* _____
is there

Wieviel *(vee-feel)* **kostet das?**_____ *Wieviel kostet das?   Wieviel kostet das?*

Jetzt, *(yets-t)* quiz yourself. See if **Sie** can translate the following thoughts into **Deutsch.**

1. Where is the telephone booth? _____

2. Where do I make a telephone call? _____

3. Where do I buy a postcard?_____

4. Where is the post office? _____

5. Where do I buy stamps? _____

6. How much is it?_____

7. Where do I send a package? _____

8. Where do I send a fax? _____

ANTWORTEN

8.	Wo sende ich ein Fax?	4.	Wo ist das Postamt?
7.	Wo sende ich ein Paket?	3.	Wo kaufe ich eine Postkarte?
6.	Wieviel kostet das?	2.	Wo mache ich einen Telefonanruf?
5.	Wo kaufe ich Briefmarken?	1.	Wo ist die Telefonzelle?

Hier sind mehr Verben.

(mah-Hen)
machen _____
to make, to do

(tsy-gen)
zeigen _____
to show

(shry-ben)
schreiben _____
to write

(beh-tsah-len)
bezahlen _____
to pay

Practice these verbs by not only filling in the blanks, but by saying them aloud many, many

times until you are comfortable with the sounds **und** the words.

(mah-Hen)
machen
to make, to do

Ich _____ einen **Anruf.** *(ahn-roof)* call

Er
Sie _____ einen **Anruf.**
Es

Wir _____ **viel.**

Sie _____ **nicht viel.**

Sie _____ **alles.** *(ahl-les)*
they   everything

(shry-ben)
schreiben
to write

Ich _____ einen **Brief.**

Er
Sie *schreibt/* _____ die **Anschrift.** *(ahn-schrift)*
Es   address

Wir _____ **viel.**

Sie _____ **nichts.** *(neeH-ts)*
you   nothing

Sie _____ ein **Fax.**

(tsy-gen)
zeigen
to show

Ich _____ **Ihnen das Buch.** *(ee-nen)*
                                       to you

Er
Sie _____ **Ihnen das Postamt.**
Es   to you

Wir _____ **Ihnen das Schloß.** *(shlohs)*
                                        castle
(post-ahmt)
Sie _____ **mir das Postamt.**
you   to me

Sie *zeigen/* _____ **mir die Straße.** *(shtrah-suh)*
                to me   street

(beh-tsah-len)
bezahlen
to pay (for)

Ich _____ die **Rechnung.** *(rehH-noong)*
                                     bill

Er
Sie _____ die **Karten.**
Es   tickets

Wir _____ die **Zugkarten.** *(tsook-kar-ten)*
                                      train tickets
(price)
Sie _____ den **Preis.**
                                    price
(kohn-tsairt-kar-ten)
Sie _____ die **Konzertkarten.**
they   concert tickets

☐ **singen** *(zing-en)*	to sing	_____
☐ **sitzen** *(zit-tsen)*	to sit	_____
☐ **der Ski** *(she)*	ski	**S** _____
☐ **die Socken** *(zoh-ken)*	socks	_____
☐ **der Sommer** *(zoh-mair)*	summer	_____

Some of these signs you probably recognize, but take a couple of minutes to review them anyway.

(shtrah-suh) (geh-shpairt)
Straße gesperrt
road closed to vehicles

(tsohl)
der Zoll
customs

(ky-nuh) (ein-fahrt)
keine Einfahrt
no entrance

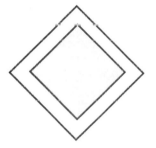

(for-fahrt) (hah-ben)
die Vorfahrt haben
main road, you have the right of way

(for-fahrt) (gay-ben)
die Vorfahrt geben
yield

(geh-shvin-deeg-kites-beh-gren-tsoong)
Geschwindigkeitsbegrenzung
speed limit

(If you can say this you've mastered
the language! Now say it quickly.)

(par-ken) (fair-boh-ten)
Parken verboten
no parking

(ew-bair-hoh-len) (fair-boh-ten)
Überholen verboten
no passing

(shtohp)
Stop
stop

(oom-lie-toong)
UMLEITUNG
detour

What follows are approximate conversions, so when you order something by liters, kilograms or grams you will have an idea of what to expect and not find yourself being handed one piece of candy when you thought you ordered an entire bag.

To Convert		Do the Math		
liters (l) to gallons,	multiply by 0.26	4 liters x 0.26	=	1.04 gallons
gallons to liters,	multiply by 3.79	10 gal. x 3.79	=	37.9 liters
kilograms (kg) to pounds,	multiply by 2.2	2 kilograms x 2.2	=	4.4 pounds
pounds to kilos,	multiply by 0.46	10 pounds x 0.46	=	4.6 kg
grams (g) to ounces,	multiply by 0.035	100 grams x 0.035	=	3.5 oz.
ounces to grams,	multiply by 28.35	10 oz. x 28.35	=	283.5 g.
meters (m) to feet,	multiply by 3.28	2 meters x 3.28	=	6.56 feet
feet to meters,	multiply by 0.3	6 feet x 0.3	=	1.8 meters

For fun, take your weight in pounds and convert it into kilograms. It sounds better that way, doesn't it? How many kilometers is it from your home to school, to work, to the post office?

The Simple Versions		
one liter	=	approximately one US quart
four liters	=	approximately one US gallon
one kilo	=	approximately 2.2 pounds
100 grams	=	approximately 3.5 ounces
500 grams	=	slightly more than one pound
one meter	=	slightly more than three feet

The distance between **New York und Frankfurt** is approximately 3,844 miles. How many kilometers would that be? It is only 790 miles between **London und Wien**. How many kilometers is that?

kilometers (km.) to miles,	multiply by 0.62	1000 km. x 0.62	=	620 miles
miles to kilometers,	multiply by 1.6	1000 miles x 1.6	=	1,600 km.

Inches	1		2		3		4		5		6		7

To convert centimeters into inches, multiply by 0.39   Example: 9 cm. x 0.39 = 3.51 in.

To convert inches into centimeters, multiply by 2.54   Example: 4 in. x 2.54 = 10.16 cm.

cm 1	2	3	4	5	6	7	8	9	10	11	12	13	14	15	16	17	18

Ja, es gibt auch *(gipt)* bills to pay **in Deutschland. Sie haben** just finished your **Abendessen und** *(ah-bent-ess-en)*
there are also / evening meal

Sie möchten die Rechnung. *(rehH-noong)* **Was machen Sie?** *(vahs) (mah-Hen)* **Sie** call for **den Kellner (Herr Ober!) oder die** *(kel-nair) (oh-bair)*
would like / bill / do you do / waiter

Kellnerin (Fräulein!). *(kel-nair-in)* **Der Kellner** will normally reel off what **Sie haben** eaten while writing
waitress

rapidly. **Er** will then place **ein Stück Papier** *(shtewk)* **auf den Tisch,** *(owf)* und say „Das macht siebzig *(mahHt)*
makes

Euro." **Sie** will pay the waiter **oder** perhaps **Sie** will pay **an der Kasse.** *(kah-suh)*
cashier

Being a seasoned traveler, **Sie** know that tipping as **Sie** may know it **in Amerika ist nicht** the

the same **in Deutschland.** Generally, **die Bedienung ist** *(beh-dee-noong)* included **in den Preisen.** *(pry-zen)* When the
service / prices

service is not included in the **Rechnung,** round the bill up **oder** simply leave what you consider
bill

an appropriate amount for your **Kellner auf dem Tisch.** When **Sie** dine out on your **Reise,** *(ry-zuh)* it
trip

may be a good idea to make a reservation. It can be difficult to get into a popular **Restaurant.**

Nevertheless, the experience is well worth the trouble **Sie** might encounter to obtain a reservation.

Und remember, **Sie** know enough **Deutsch** to make a reservation. Just speak slowly and clearly.

❑	**die Sonne** *(zoh-nuh)*	sun
❑	**die Spezialität** *(shpay-tsee-ah-lih-tate)*	specialty
❑	**das Spanien** *(shpah-nee-en)*	Spain
	— **wo sie Spanisch sprechen** *(shpah-nish)*	
❑	**der Sport** *(shport)*	sport

S

Remember these key **Wörter** when dining out **in Deutschland,** *(uh-stair-rike)* **Österreich oder in der Schweiz.** *(shvites)*
Austria   Switzerland

(kel-nair)
der Kellner _____
waiter

(kel-nair-in)
die Kellnerin _____
waitress

(rehH-noong)
die Rechnung   *die Rechnung* _____
bill

(trink-gelt)
das Trinkgeld _____
tip

(shpy-zuh-kar-tuh)
die Speisekarte _____
menu

(kvih-toong)
die Quittung _____
receipt

(ent-shool-dee-goong)
Entschuldigung _____
excuse me

(dahn-kuh)
danke _____
thank you

(bit-tuh)
bitte _____
please

(gay-ben) (zee) (mir)
Geben Sie mir . . . _____
give   me

(kohn-vair-zah-tsee-ohn)
Hier ist a sample **Konversation** involving paying **die Rechnung** when leaving a **Hotel.**
(rehH-noong)
bill

(yoh-hah-nes)
Johannes: *(ent-shool-dee-goong)* **Entschuldigung. Ich möchte die Rechnung** *(rehH-noong)* **bezahlen.** *(beh-tsah-len)*

_____ *Entschuldigung. Ich möchte die Rechnung bezahlen.* _____

Hotelmanager: *(vel-Hes)* **Welches Zimmer, bitte?**
which   room

_____

Johannes: **Zimmer dreihundertzehn.**

_____

Hotelmanager: **Danke.** *(eye-nen)* **Einen Moment, bitte.**

_____

Hotelmanager: **Hier ist die** *(rehH-noong)* **Rechnung.**

_____

If **Sie** have any *(pro-blame-uh)* **Probleme mit den Nummern,** just ask someone to write out **die Nummern** so

Sie can be sure you understand everything correctly,

(shry-ben)
„**Bitte,** **schreiben Sie die Nummern** *(owf)* **auf! Danke.**"
please   write out

Practice: _____
(Please write out the numbers. Thank you.)

☐ **der Staat** *(shtaht)* . . . . state, country _____
☐ **der Student** *(shtoo-dent)* . . . . student (male) _____
☐ **die Studentin** *(shtoo-dent-in)* . . . . student (female) **S** _____
☐ **der Sturm** *(shturm)* . . . . storm _____
☐ **das Südamerika** *(zewt-ah-mair-ih-kah)* . . . . South America _____

Nun, let's take a break from **die Rechnungen** *(rehH-noong-en)* **und das Geld** *(gelt)* **und** learn some fun, **neue** *(noy-uh)* **Wörter.**

bills — money — new

Sie can always practice these **Wörter** by using your flash cards at the back of this **Buch.** Carry these flash cards in your purse, pocket, briefcase **oder** knapsack **und** *use them!*

(owf) **auf** open

_____

(tsoo) **zu** closed

_____

(grohs) **groß** big

_____

(kline) **klein** small

_____

(geh-zoont) **gesund** healthy

_____

(krahnk) **krank** sick

_____

(goot) **gut** good

_____

(shlehHt) **schlecht** bad

_____

(hice) **heiß** hot

_____

(kahlt) **kalt** cold

_____

☐ **die Suppe** *(zoo-puh)* . . . . soup
☐ **die Symphonie** *(zoom-foh-nee)* . . . . symphony   **s** _____

In the following **Wörter,** notice how often the initial „**T**" becomes a "D" in English.

☐ **der Tag** *(tahk)* . . . . day   **t** _____
☐ **der Tanz** *(tahn-ts)* . . . . dance   _____

71

(koorts)
kurz _____
short

(lahng)
lang _____
long

(lahng-zahm)
langsam _____
slow

(shnel)
schnell _____
fast

(hohH)
hoch _____
tall, high

(nee-drig)
niedrig _____
low

(ahlt)
alt _____
old

(yoong)
jung _____
young

(toy-air)
teuer _____
expensive

(bil-lig)
billig _____
inexpensive

(rike)
reich _____
rich

(arm)
arm _____
poor

(feel)
viel _____
a lot

(vay-nig)
wenig _____
a little

☐ **tanzen** *(tahn-tsen)* .... to dance
☐ **die Tochter** *(tohH-tair)* .... daughter
☐ **träumen** *(troy-men)* .... to dream
☐ **tun** *(toon)* .... to do
☐ **die Tür** *(tewr)* .... door

t

_____
_____
_____
_____
_____

Hier sind die neuen Verben. *(noy-en)*

(viss-en)
wissen _____
to know (fact)

(kuh-nen)
können _____
to be able to, can

(lay-zen)
lesen _____
to read

(mew-sen)
müssen _____
to have to, must

Study the patterns below closely, as **Sie** will use these verbs a lot.

(viss-en)
wissen
to know

Adenauerstr. 15

Ich __weiß/_____ alles.
(ahl-les) everything

Er
Sie __weiß/_____ die Anschrift.
Es
address

Wir __wissen/_____ , wie alt er ist.
(vee) *(air)*

Sie _____ , wo das Hotel ist.
you *(voh)*

Sie _____ nichts.
(neeH-ts)

(kuh-nen)
können
to be able to, can

Ich kann Deutsch sprechen.

Ich __kann/_____ Deutsch sprechen.
(shpreh-Hen)

Er
Sie __kann/_____ Deutsch lesen.
Es
(lay-zen) read

Wir __können/_____ Englisch sprechen.

Sie _____ Deutsch verstehen.
(fair-shtay-en)

Sie _____ Italienisch sprechen.
they *(ee-tah-lee-ay-nish)*

(lay-zen)
lesen
to read

Ich __lese/_____ das Buch.
(booH)

Er
Sie __liest/_____ die Zeitschrift.
Es
(tsight-shrift) magazine

Wir __lesen/_____ wenig.
(vay-nig)

Sie _____ viel.
(feel) a lot

Sie _____ die Zeitung.
they newspaper

(mew-sen)
müssen
to have to, must

Ich __muß/_____ Deutsch lernen.
(lair-nen)

Er
Sie __muß/_____ das Buch lesen.
Es
(lay-zen)

Wir __müssen/_____ das Schloß sehen.
(shlohs) *(zay-en)* castle

Sie _____ einen Brief schreiben.
you *(shry-ben)*

Sie _____ die Rechnung bezahlen.
(rehH-noong)

❏	die Uniform *(oo-nee-form)*	uniform	
❏	das Ungarn *(oon-garn)*	Hungary	**u**
	— wo sie Ungarisch sprechen *(oon-gar-ish)*		
❏	uninteressant *(oon-in-tair-es-sahnt)*	uninteresting	
❏	die Universität *(oo-nih-vair-zih-tate)*	university	

Notice that **"können" und "müssen"** along with **"möchte"** and **"möchten"** can be combined

with another verb. **"Wissen"** is a bit different *(ah-bair)* **aber** **sehr wichtig.**
but

Ich *(vice)* **weiß,** wo die Bank ist. know	
Ich **weiß nicht.** do not know	

Wir *(kuh-nen)* **können** das Buch *(lay-zen)* **lesen.** can	
Wir **können** einen Brief **senden.**	

Sie *(moos)* **muß** schlafen. must/has to sleep
Sie **muß** bezahlen. she

Ich *(vice)* **weiß** die Antwort.
know
Ich *(kahn)* **kann** Deutsch sprechen.
can
Ich *(moos)* **muß** Deutsch sprechen.
must
Ich *(murk-tuh)* **möchte** Deutsch sprechen.
would like

Können Sie translate the sentences **unten** into **Deutsch?**
can

1. I can speak German. _____

2. They must pay the bill. _____

3. He has to pay the bill. _____

4. We know the answers. ___Wir wissen die Antworten. Wir wissen die Antworten.___

5. She knows a lot. _____

6. We can read German. _____

7. I cannot find the hotel. _____

8. We are not able to (cannot) understand German. _____

9. I would like to see Munich. _____

10. She can write a postcard. _____

74

Jetzt, draw **Linien** between the opposites **unten.** Do not forget to say them out loud. Say these
(lines)

Wörter every day to describe **Dinge in Ihrem Haus, in der Schule oder** at work.
(ear-em) *(dair)* *(shoo-luh)*
your *home* *school*

(grohs)
groß

links

(yoong)
jung

arm

(krahnk)
krank

(lahng)
lang

(feel)
viel

(goot)
gut

(hice)
heiß

(oon-ten)
unten

(lahng-zahm)
langsam

(toy-air)
teuer

(tsoo)
zu

(oh-ben)
oben

(owf)
auf

(koorts)
kurz

billig

(vay-nig)
wenig

(geh-zoont)
gesund

schnell

(ahlt)
alt

klein

(rehH-ts)
rechts

(kahll)
kalt

(rike)
reich

(shlehHt)
schlecht

❑	**der Untergrund** *(oon-tair-groont)*	underground, subway	
❑	**unten** *(oon-ten)*	downstairs	
❑	**unter** *(oon-tair)*	under	**u**
❑	**unterwegs** *(oon-tair-vehgs)*	in transit, on the way	
❑	**die Unterwelt** *(oon-tair-velt)*	underworld	

Reisen, Reisen, Reisen
(ry-zen) (ry-zen) (ry-zen)
to travel

Gestern nach München! *(mewn-shen)*
yesterday

Heute nach Hamburg! *(hahm-boorg)*
today

Morgen nach Berlin! *(bair-leen)*
tomorrow

If you know a few key **Wörter,** traveling can be very easy in German-speaking countries.

Deutschland ist nicht sehr groß, in fact, it is approximately **so groß wie Oregon und** *(zair)* *(grohs)* *(zoh)* *(vee)*
large

Washington zusammen. Das macht das Reisen sehr einfach. Wie reisen Sie? *(tsoo-zah-men)* *(ry-zen)* *(ein-fahH)* *(vee)* *(ry-zen)*
together   simple, easy

Helene reist mit dem Flugzeug. *(flook-tsoyk)*
airplane

Hermine reist mit dem Schiff. *(shif)*
boat

Annette reist mit dem Motorrad. *(moh-tor-raht)*

Anita reist mit dem Zug. *(tsook)*

Hans reist mit dem Auto. *(ry-st)* *(dehm)*
travels

Karl reist mit dem Bus. *(boos)*

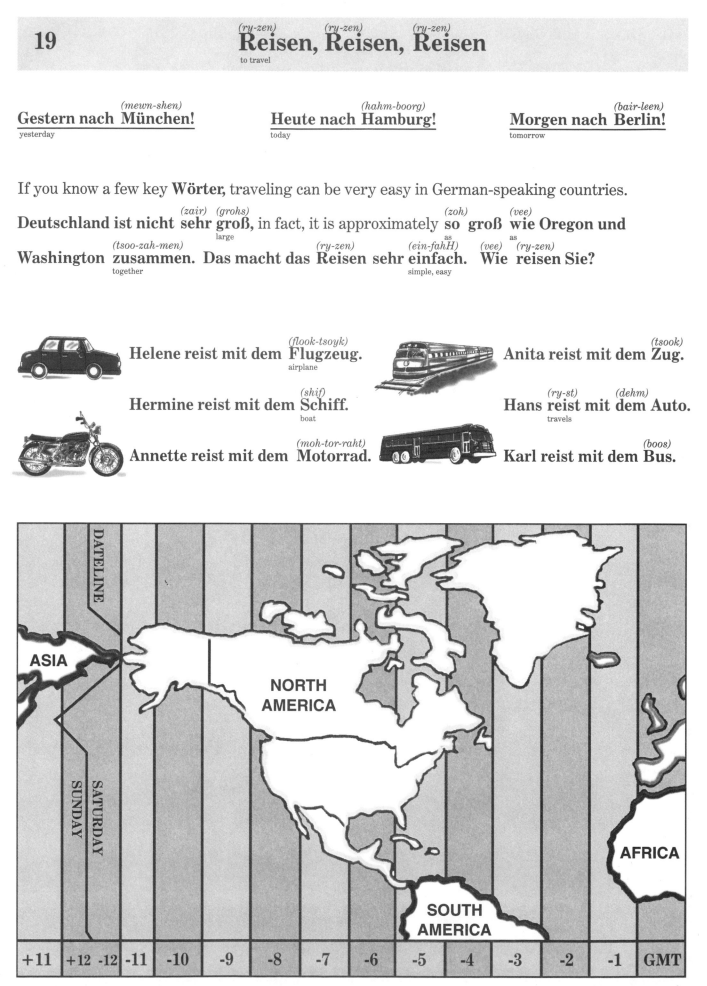

| +11 | +12 | -12 | -11 | -10 | -9 | -8 | -7 | -6 | -5 | -4 | -3 | -2 | -1 | GMT |

When **Sie** are traveling, **Sie** will want to tell others your nationality **und Sie** will meet people from all corners of the world. Can you guess where someone is from if they say one of the following? **Die Antworten** are in your glossary beginning on page 108.

Ich komme aus England. *(ows) (eng-lahnt)* _____
come   from

Ich komme aus Italien. *(ee-tah-lee-en)* _____
come   from

Ich komme aus Frankreich. *(frahnk-rike)* _____
from

Ich komme aus Spanien. *(shpah-nee-en)* _____

Ich komme aus Belgien. *(bel-gee-en)* _____

Ich komme aus der Schweiz. *(dair) (shvites)* _____

Ich komme aus Polen. *(poh-len)* _____

Ich komme aus Dänemark. *(day-nuh-mark)* _____

Ich komme aus Österreich. *(uh-stair-rike)* _____

Wir kommen aus Norwegen. *(nor-vay-gen)* _____
we   come

Wir kommen aus Schweden. *(shvay-den)* _____
we   come

Wir kommen aus der Slowakei. *(sloh-vah-kai)* _____

Wir kommen aus Ungarn. *(oon-garn)* _____

Er kommt aus Holland. *(hohl-lahnt)* _____
he   comes

Er kommt aus Tschechien. *(cheh-Hee-en)* _____

Sie kommt aus Rußland. *(roos-lahnt)* _____
she   comes

Sie kommt aus Südafrika. *(zewt-ah-frih-kah)* _____

Ich komme aus Kanada. *(kah-nah-dah)* _____

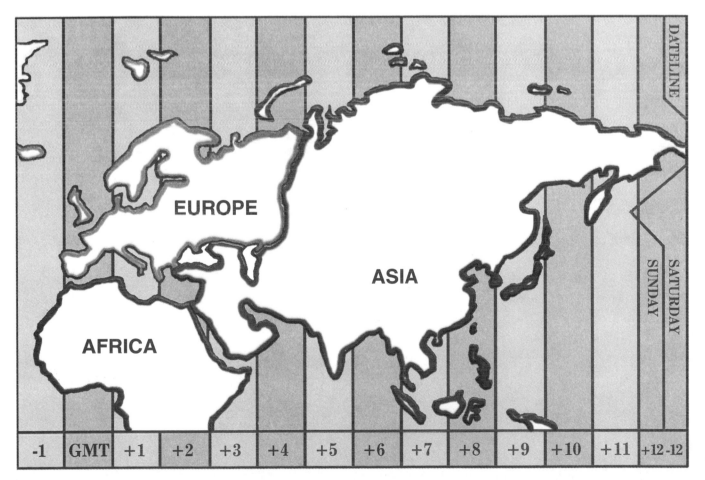

| -1 | GMT | +1 | +2 | +3 | +4 | +5 | +6 | +7 | +8 | +9 | +10 | +11 | +12 -12 |

Die Deutschen *(doy-chen)* love to travel, so **es ist** no surprise to find many **Wörter** built on the **Wort**
Germans

„**Reisen**" *(ry-zen)* which can mean either "trip" **oder** "to travel." Practice saying the following **Wörter**

many times. **Sie** will see them **oft.** *(ohft)*
often

reisen *(ry-zen)* _____
to travel

das Reisebüro *(ry-zuh-bew-roh)* _____
travel agency

der Reisende *(ry-zen-duh)* _____
traveler

Gute Reise! *(goo-tuh) (ry-zuh)* _____
have a good trip

If **Sie** choose to travel **mit dem Auto,** here are a few key **Wörter.**

die Autobahn *(ow-toh-bahn)* _____
freeway

die Einfahrt *(ein-fahrt)* _____
entrance for a vehicle

die Straße *(shtrah-suh)* _____
street, road

die Ausfahrt *(ows-fahrt)* _____
exit for a vehicle

der Mietwagen *(meet-vah-gen)* _____
rental car

die Tankstelle *(tahnk-shtel-luh)* _____
service station

Unten sind some basic signs which **Sie** should **auch** learn to recognize quickly. **Gang** *(gahng)* comes from

the verb **gehen** meaning "to go" **oder** "to walk." That should help you **mit diesen Wörtern.** *(dee-zen)*
these

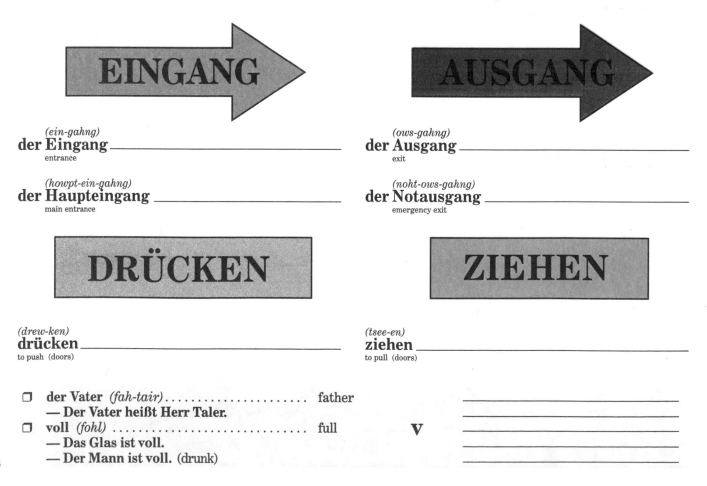

der Eingang *(ein-gahng)* _____
entrance

der Ausgang *(ows-gahng)* _____
exit

der Haupteingang *(howpt-ein-gahng)* _____
main entrance

der Notausgang *(noht-ows-gahng)* _____
emergency exit

drücken *(drew-ken)* _____
to push (doors)

ziehen *(tsee-en)* _____
to pull (doors)

❏ **der Vater** *(fah-tair)* . . . . father
    — Der Vater heißt Herr Taler.

❏ **voll** *(fohl)* . . . . full
    — Das Glas ist voll.
    — Der Mann ist voll. (drunk)

v _____
_____
_____
_____

78

Let's learn the basic travel verbs. Take out a piece of paper **und** make up your own sentences

with these **neuen Wörtern.** _(noy-en)_ _(vur-tairn)_ Follow the same pattern **Sie haben** in previous Steps.

(flee-gen)
fliegen _____
to fly

(ahn-koh-men)
ankommen _____
to arrive

(ahp-fah-ren)
abfahren _____
to leave, depart

(gipt)
es gibt _____
there is, there are

(zit-tsen)
sitzen _____
to sit

(fah-ren)
fahren _____
to drive, to travel by vehicle

(pah-ken)
packen _____
to pack

(oom-shty-gen)
umsteigen _____
to transfer (vehicles)

Hier sind mehr neue Wörter für die Reise.

(flook-hah-fen)
der Flughafen
airport

(bahn-shtaig)
der Bahnsteig
platform

(far-plahn)
der Fahrplan
timetable

Von Berlin nach Leipzig		
Abfahrt	Zug Nr.	Ankunft
04:13	567	06:13
09:42	1433	11:45
12:40	1892	15:00
15:10	32	17:30
19:19	650	21:50

(bahn-hohf)
der Bahnhof
train station

❏ **die Vereinigten Staaten** _(fair-eye-neeg-ten)(shtah-ten)_ United States _____
— **Ich wohne in den Vereinigten Staaten.**
— **Ich komme aus den Vereinigten Staaten.** **V** _____
❏ **das Volk** _(folk)_ . . . . folk, people _____
— **das deutsche Volk** _____

Mit diesen Wörtern, Sie sind ready for any **Reise**, anywhere. **Sie** should have no **Probleme**
(dee-zen) / these

mit these new verbs, just remember the basic "plug-in" formula **Sie haben** already learned. Use

that knowledge to translate the following thoughts into **Deutsch**. **Die Antworten sind unten.**

1. I fly to Berlin. _____

2. I drive to Bonn. _____

3. He travels by (with the) train to Heidelberg. _____

4. We sit in the airplane. _____

5. We buy three tickets to Frankfurt. _____

6. They travel to Salzburg. _____

7. Where is the train to Vienna? _____

8. How do we fly to Germany? With Lufthansa or with Swiss Air? _____

_____

Hier sind some **wichtige Wörter für Reisende.**
(ry-zen-duh) / travelers

Von Innsbruck nach München		
Abfahrt	**Zug Nr.**	**Ankunft**
08:32	118	11:46
11:35	413	14:52
14:11	718	17:52
18:12	1132	22:53
Gute Reise!		

(beh-zets-t)
besetzt _____
occupied

(fry)
frei _____
free

(ahp-tile)
das Abteil _____
compartment, wagon

(plahts)
der Platz _____
seat

(ahp-fahrt)
die Abfahrt _____
departure

(ahn-koonft)
die Ankunft _____
arrival

(ows-lahnt)
das Ausland _____
foreign

(in-lahnt)
das Inland _____
domestic, internal (of the country)

Increase your travel **Wörter** by writing out **die Wörter unten und** practicing the sample sentences out loud. Practice asking *(frah-gen)* **Fragen mit „wo.“** It will help you later.

(nahH)
nach _____
to
Wo ist der Zug nach Dresden?

(glice)
das Gleis _____
track
Wo ist Gleis Nummer sieben?

(foont bew-roh)
das Fundbüro _____
lost-and-found office
Gibt es ein Fundbüro?

(bahn-shtaig)
der Bahnsteig _____
platform
Wo ist Bahnsteig fünf-A?

(flook)
der Flug _____
flight
Wo ist der Flug nach Innsbruck?

(plahts)
der Platz _____
seat
Ist dieser Platz frei?

(veck-zel-shtoo-buh)
die Wechselstube _____
money-exchange office
Gibt es eine Wechselstube?

(shahl-tair)
der Schalter _____
counter
Wo ist Schalter Nummer acht?

(var-tuh-zahl)
der Wartesaal _____
waiting room
Gibt es einen Wartesaal?

(shpy-zuh-vah-gen)
der Speisewagen _____
dining car
Gibt es einen Speisewagen?

(shlahf-vah-gen)
der Schlafwagen _____
sleeping car
Gibt es einen Schlafwagen?

(lee-guh-vah-gen)
der Liegewagen _____
car with berths
Wo ist der Liegewagen?

_____ (when) _____ (when) **kommt der Zug** *(tsook)* **an?** arrives

_____ (what) _____ (what) **ist los?** *(lohs)*

☐ **von** *(fohn)* .... from
— **Die Frau kommt von Frankfurt.**

☐ **vor** *(for)* .... before, in front of

☐ **der Vorname** *(for-nah-muh)* .... first name, given name
— **Der Vater heißt Helmut mit Vornamen.**

Können Sie the following **lesen?** *(lay-zen)*
can

← **Sie sitzen nun in dem Flugzeug und Sie**

(flee-gen)
fliegen nach Deutschland. Sie haben das

(pahs)
Geld, die Fahrkarten und den Paß. Sie
passport

sind nun Tourist. Sie landen morgen

(shpahs)
in Deutschland. Gute Reise! Viel Spaß!

(tsue-guh)
Deutsche Züge come in many shapes, sizes, **und** speeds. **Es gibt** *(gipt)* **Personenzüge** *(pair-zoh-nen-tsue-guh)* (**sehr**
trains   there are

langsam), Eilzüge *(ile-tsue-guh)* **(langsam), Schnellzüge** *(shnel-tsue-guh)* **(schnell), und Inter-City Züge** *(in-tair)* *(tsue-guh)* **(sehr schnell).**

If **Sie** plan to travel a long distance, **Sie** may wish to catch an Inter-City train or **TEE (Trans-**

Europa-Express) which travels faster **und** makes fewer intermediate stops.

☐ **das Wasser** *(vah-sair)*	water		_____
☐ **der Westen** *(ves-ten)*	West	**W**	_____
☐ **das Wild** *(vilt)*	venison, game		_____
☐ **der Wein** *(vine)*	wine		_____
☐ **der Wind** *(vint)*	wind		_____

Knowing these travel **Wörter** will make your holiday twice as enjoyable **und** at least three times as easy. Review these **Reisewörter** by doing the crossword puzzle **unten**. Drill yourself on this Step by selecting other destinations **und** ask your own **Fragen** about **Züge, Busse, oder Flugzeuge** *(flook-tsoy-guh)* that go there. Select more **neue Wörter** from your **Wörterbuch und** ask your own **Fragen** beginning with **wann, wo und wieviel**. **Die Antworten** to the crossword puzzle are at the bottom of the next page.

ACROSS
1. sleeping car
2. yesterday
3. with
4. bus
5. occupied
6. I
7. to, towards
8. to pack
9. passport
10. and
11. to travel
12. domestic
13. to sit
14. nothing
15. exit (for people)
16. to drive, go
17. train

DOWN
1. restaurant
2. money
3. to rain
4. airport
5. rental car
6. clock, time
7. ship
8. dining car
9. track
10. now
12. train station
13. place, seat
14. foreign

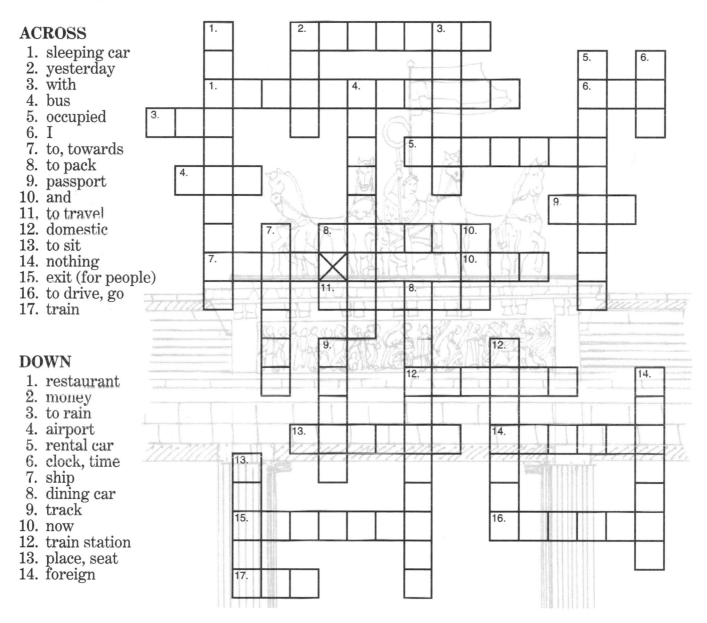

Das Brandenburger Tor stands on the old boundary between East and West Berlin. This neo-classical landmark was rebuilt in 1791 and rises to a height of 65 feet.

☐ **der Winter** *(vin-tair)* .... winter _____
☐ **der Wolle** *(voh-luh)* .... wool _____
☐ **das Willkommen** *(vil-koh-men)* .... welcome **W** _____
☐ **wandern** *(vahn-dairn)* .... to wander, hike _____
☐ **die Waren** *(vah-ren)* .... wares, goods _____

83

What about inquiring about **Preisen?** **Sie** *(kuh-nen)* **können das** *(owH)* **auch** *(frah-gen)* **fragen.**
prices   can   ask

(vahs)
Was kostet eine Karte nach *(hi-del-bairg)* **Heidelberg?** _____

(vahs)
Was kostet eine Karte nach *(veen)* **Wien?** _____
Vienna

(vahs)
Was kostet eine Karte nach *(koh-pen-hah-gen)* **Kopenhagen?** _____

(ein-fahH)
einfach _____
one-way

(hin) *(oont)* *(tsoo-rewk)*
hin und zurück _____
round-trip

What about   *(ahp-fahrt)* **Abfahrt und** *(ahn-koonft)* **Ankunft** times? **Sie** *(kuh-nen)* **können das** *(dahs)* **auch fragen.**
     departure   arrival

(vahn) *(fleegt)* *(flook-tsoyk)* *(rohm)* *(ahp)*
Wann fliegt das Flugzeug nach Rom ab? _____
departs   Rome

(fairt) *(tsook)* *(prahg)*
Wann fährt der Zug nach Prag ab? _____
departs   Prague

(fairt) *(mar-boorg)*
Wann fährt der Zug nach Marburg ab? _____

(ows) *(bair-leen)* *(ahn)*
Wann kommt der Zug aus Berlin an? _____
arrives   from

(flook-tsoyk) *(zahlts-boorg)*
Wann kommt das Flugzeug aus Salzburg an? _____
flight

Sie have just arrived **in Deutschland. Sie sind nun** *(ahm)* **am** *(bahn-hohf)* **Bahnhof. Wo** do you wish to go?
                 at the

Nach München? Nach Nürnberg? Tell that to the person at the *(shahl-tair)* **Schalter** selling **Karten!**
                                         counter

(murk-tuh)
Ich möchte nach Innsbruck fahren. _____
                to travel, go

(vahn) *(fairt)* *(tsook)*
Wann fährt der Zug nach Innsbruck? _____

(vahs)
Was kostet eine Karte nach Innsbruck? _____

Now that **Sie** know the words essential for traveling **in Deutschland,** *(uh-stair-rike)* **Österreich oder in der**

(shvites)
Schweiz, what are some specialty items **Sie** might go in search of?

(vy-nuh)
Weine
wines

(ahn-denk-en)
Andenken
souvenirs

(shoh-koh-lah-den)
Schokoladen
chocolates

(beer-shty-nuh)
Biersteine
beer mugs

(vy-nahHts-geh-shen-kuh)
Weihnachtsgeschenke
Christmas presents

(koo-kooks-oor)
die Kuckucksuhr
cuckoo clock

Consider using GERMAN *a language map*™ as well. GERMAN *a language map*™ is the perfect

companion for your travels when **Sie** may not wish to take along this **Buch.** Each section

focuses on essentials for your **Reise.** Your *Language Map*™ is not meant to replace learning

Deutsch, but will help you in the event **Sie** forget something and need a little bit of help. For

more information about the *Language Map*™ Series, please turn to page 132.

☐ **warm** *(varm)*	warm	
☐ **die Warnung** *(var-noong)*	warning	
☐ **wünschen** *(vewn-shen)*	to wish	**W**
— Was wünschen Sie?		
☐ **der Weg** *(veg)*	way	

20   Die Speisekarte
(shpy-zuh-kar-tuh)
menu

Sie sind nun in Deutschland und Sie haben ein *(hoh-tel-tsih-mair)* **Hotelzimmer. Sie haben** *(hoong-air)* **Hunger. Wo gibt es**
is there

ein *(goo-tes)* **gutes Restaurant?** First of all, **es gibt** different types of places to eat. Let's learn them.
there are

das Gasthaus *(gahst-house)*

an inn with a full range of meals

das Café *(kah-fay)*

a coffee shop with pastries, snacks **und** beverages;
this should be a regular stop every day about 3:30 pm.

der Schnellimbiß *(shnel-im-biss)*

a snack bar, specializing in **Wurst und** beverages

die Weinstube *(vine-shtoo-buh)*

a small, cozy restaurant specializing in **Weine** with some hot dishes, cheeses, **und** snacks

der Ratskeller *(rahts-kel-air)*

a restaurant frequently found in the basement of **das Rathaus**

If **Sie** look around you **in einem deutschen Restaurant, Sie** will see that some customs might be

different from yours. Sharing *(tish-uh)* **Tische mit** others **ist** a common **und sehr** pleasant custom.
tables

Before beginning your meal, be sure to wish those sharing your table – „ *(goo-ten)* **Guten** *(ah-peh-teet)* **Appetit!"**
enjoy your meal

Your turn to practice now.

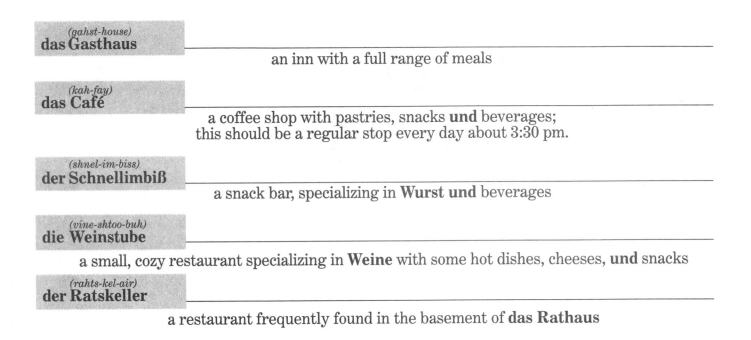

_____
(enjoy your meal)

And at least one more time for practice!

_____
(enjoy your meal)

☐ **der Zentimeter** *(tsen-tih-may-tair)* . . . . centimeter   _____
☐ **das Zentrum** *(tsen-troom)* . . . . center   _____
☐ **die Zeremonie** *(tsair-eh-moh-nee)* . . . . ceremony   **Z**   _____
☐ **die Zigarette** *(tsih-gah-ret-tuh)* . . . . cigarette   _____
☐ **die Zigarre** *(tsih-gah-ruh)* . . . . cigar   _____

Start imagining now all the new taste treats you will experience abroad. Try all of the different

types of eating establishments mentioned on the previous page. Experiment. If **Sie finden ein**

Restaurant that **Sie möchten** to try, consider calling ahead to make a **Reservierung.**
(rez-air-veer-oong)
reservation

(rez-air-veer-en)
„Ich möchte einen Tisch reservieren." If **Sie brauchen eine Speisekarte,** catch the attention
reserve   *(brow-Hen)*   *(shpy-zuh-kar-tuh)*
     need

of the **Kellner,** saying

> *(hair)*   *(oh-bair)*   *(shpy-zuh-kar-tuh)*
> **Herr Ober! Die Speisekarte, bitte.**

_____

(Waiter. The menu, please.)

If your **Kellner** asks if **Sie** enjoyed your

(ess-en)   *(dahn-kuh)*
Essen, a smile **und** a **„Ja, danke"** will tell him
meal

that you did.

(doy-chuh)   *(res-toh-rahnts)*   *(shpy-zuh-kar-tuh)*
Most **deutsche Restaurants** post **die Speisekarte** outside **oder** inside. Do not hesitate to ask to

                         (viss-en)   *(pry-zen)*
see **die Speisekarte** before being seated so **Sie wissen** what type of meals **und Preisen Sie** will
                      know   *prices*

                        (tah-ges-geh-reeHt)   *(men-ew)*
encounter. Most **Restaurants** offer **ein Tagesgericht oder ein Menü**. These are complete
                         daily special   *special meal*

(price)
meals at a fair **Preis.**
price

❐	**der Zirkus** *(tseer-koos)*	circus	
❐	**die Zivilisation** *(tsih-vih-lih-zah-tsee-ohn)* . .	civilization	
❐	**der Zoo** *(tsoh)*	zoo	**Z**
❐	**zu** *(tsoo)*	to	
❐	**der Zucker** *(tsoo-kair)*	sugar	

In Deutschland gibt es drei main meals to enjoy every day, plus perhaps **Kaffee und Kuchen** *(kah-fay)* *(koo-Hen)* cake

(fewr)
für the tired traveler in the **späten** Nachmittag. *(shpay-ten)* late

(frew-shtewk)
das Frühstück _____
breakfast

In Hotels und Pensionen this meal may start as early as 6:00 and finish at 8:00. *(pahn-see-oh-nen)* guest houses

Check serving times before **Sie** retire for the night or you might miss out!

(mit-tahk-ess-en)
das Mittagessen _____
mid-day meal, lunch

generally served from 11:30 to 14:00; you will be able to find any type of meal, **groß oder klein,** served at this time. For most people, this **ist** the main meal of the day.

(ah-bent-ess-en)
das Abendessen _____
evening meal, dinner

generally served from 18:00 to 20:30 and sometimes later; frequently after 21:30, only cold snacks **oder heiße** Wurst are served in **Restaurants** *(hi-suh)*

Nun for a preview of delights to come . . . At the back of this **Buch, Sie** will find a sample

deutsche Speisekarte. Lesen Sie die Speisekarte heute und lernen Sie die neuen Wörter. *(lay-zen)* read *(hoy-tuh)* today *(lair-nen)* learn

When **Sie** are ready to leave on your **Reise,** cut out **die Speisekarte,** fold it, **und** carry it in your

pocket, wallet **oder** purse. Before you go, how do **Sie** say these **drei** phrases which are so very

important for the hungry traveler?

Excuse me. I would like to reserve a table. _____

Waiter! The menu, please. _____

Enjoy your meal! _____

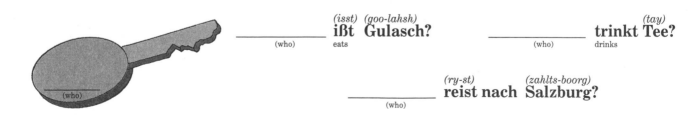

_____ **ißt Gulasch?**   _____ **trinkt Tee?**
(who)   *(isst)* *(goo-lahsh)* eats   (who)   *(tay)* drinks

_____ **reist nach Salzburg?**
(who)   *(ry-st)* *(zahlts-boorg)*

_____
(who)

Learning the following should help you to identify what **Sie** have ordered **und wie** it will be prepared.
- ☐ **vom Rind** *(fohm)(rint)* . . . . beef _____
- ☐ **vom Kalb** *(kahlp)* . . . . veal _____
- ☐ **vom Schwein** *(shvine)* . . . . pork _____
- ☐ **vom Hammel** *(hah-mel)* . . . . mutton _____

Die Speisekarte unten hat the main categories **Sie** will find in most restaurants. Learn them **heute** so that **Sie** will easily recognize them when you dine **in** *(bair-leen)* **Berlin oder in** *(veen)* **Wien.** Be sure to write the words in the blanks below.

Vienna

(shpy-zuh-kar-tuh)
die Speisekarte

(for-shpy-zen)
Vorspeisen
appetizers

(zoo-pen)
Suppen
soups

(eye-air-shpy-zon)
Eierspeisen
egg dishes

(fish-geh-reeH-tuh)
Fischgerichte
fish dishes

(howpt-geh-reeH-tuh)
Hauptgerichte
entrees, main meals

Grill- und *(fahn-en-geh-reeH-tuh)* **Pfannengerichte**
grilled and fried food

(geh-mew-zuh)
Gemüse
vegetables

(zah-lah-tuh)
Salate
salads

(nahH-tish)
Nachtisch
dessert

(kahl-tuh) (shpy-zen)
Kalte Speisen
cold meals (plates of cheese and cold cuts)

(ice)
Eis
ice cream

(koo-Hen)
Kuchen
pastries, cake

(geh-trenk-uh)
Getränke
beverages

☐	**vom Lamm** *(lahm)*	lamb	_____
☐	**das Geflügel** *(geh-flew-gel)*	poultry	_____
☐	**das Wild** *(wilt)*	game	_____
☐	**gebraten** *(geh-brah-ten)*	roasted, fried	_____
☐	**im Backteig** *(bahk-taig)*	in batter	_____

Sie may also order **Gemüse** *(geh-mew-zuh)* **und Kartoffeln** *(kar-toh-feln)* **mit** your **Essen und einen gemischten** *(geh-mish-ten)* **Salat.** *(zah-laht)*

vegetables   potatoes   mixed

One day at an open-air **Markt** will teach you **die Namen** *(nah-men)* for all the different kinds of **Gemüse** *(geh-mew-zuh)*

market

und Obst, *(ohpst)* plus it will be a delightful experience for you. **Sie können** *(kuh-nen)* always consult your menu

fruit   can

guide at the back of this **Buch** if **Sie** forget **die richtigen Namen.** **Nun** *(noon)* **Sie** *(zee)* are seated, **und der**

Kellner kommt.

waiter

Die Speisekarte, bitte.

Und zu trinken?

Ein Glas Weißwein, bitte.

Das Frühstück *(frew-shtewk)* **ist ein bißchen** *(bis-Hen)* different because **es ist** fairly standardized **und Sie** will

breakfast   a   little

frequently take it at your **Pension,** *(pahn-see-ohn)* as **es ist** included **in dem Preis** *(price)* of the **Zimmer.** *(tsih-mair)* **Unten ist** a

sample of what **Sie können** expect to greet you **am Morgen.** *(ahm)*

in the   morning

Getränke   und . . .

ein **Kännchen Kaffee** *(ken-chen)*

pot

ein **Kännchen Tee**

ein **Kännchen Schokolade**

Orangensaft *(oh-rahn-zhen-zahft)*

orange   juice

Tomatensaft *(toh-mah-ten-zahft)*

Apfelsaft *(ahp-fel-zahft)*

apple   juice

Milch

Brot *(broht)*

Brötchen *(bruht-chen)*

Butter

Marmelade

Käse *(kay-zuh)*

Schinken *(shink-en)*

ham

ein **gekochtes Ei** *(geh-kohH-tes) (eye)*

cooked   egg

❏ **gekocht** *(geh-kohHt)* . . . . cooked, boiled   _____
❏ **gebacken** *(geh-bah-ken)* . . . . baked   _____
❏ **gegrillt** *(geh-grilt)* . . . . grilled   _____
❏ **paniert** *(pah-neart)* . . . . breaded   _____
❏ **gefüllt** *(geh-fewlt)* . . . . stuffed   _____

90

Hier ist an example of what **Sie** might select for your evening meal. Using your menu guide on pages 117 and 118, as well as what **Sie** have learned in this Step, fill in the blanks *in English* with what **Sie** believe your **Kellner** will bring you. **Die Antworten sind** below.

Vorspeisen
Westfälischer Schinken mit Bauernbrot

Suppe
Tagessuppe

Hauptgericht
Wiener Schnitzel mit Röstkartoffeln und Erbsen

Nachtisch
Eisbecher mit Früchten und Schlagsahne

(when)

(how)

(why)

Nun ist a good time for a quick review. Draw lines between **die deutschen Wörter und** their English equivalents.

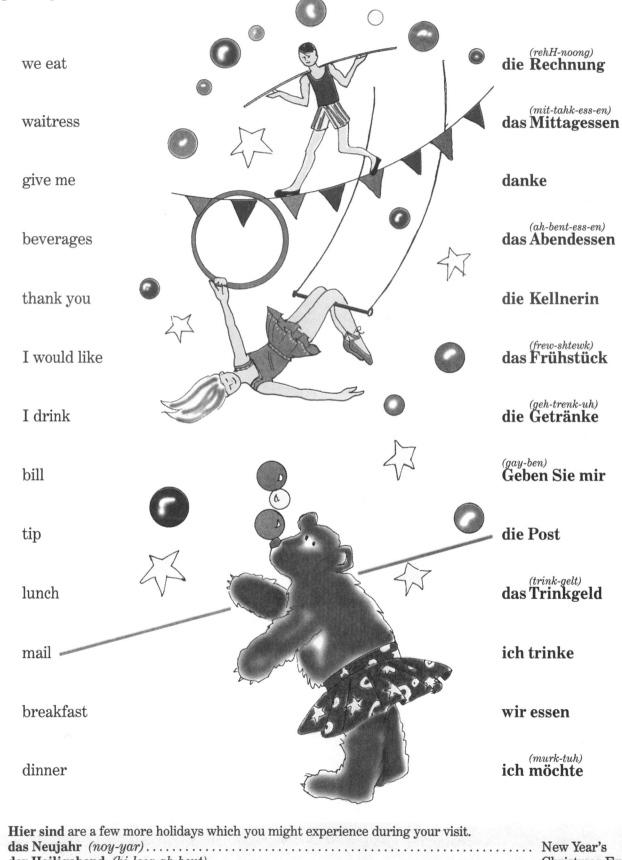

we eat

waitress

give me

beverages

thank you

I would like

I drink

bill

tip

lunch

mail

breakfast

dinner

(rehH-noong)
die **Rechnung**

(mit-tahk-ess-en)
das **Mittagessen**

danke

(ah-bent-ess-en)
das **Abendessen**

die **Kellnerin**

(frew-shtewk)
das **Frühstück**

(geh-trenk-uh)
die **Getränke**

(gay-ben)
Geben Sie mir

die **Post**

(trink-gelt)
das **Trinkgeld**

ich trinke

wir essen

(murk-tuh)
ich **möchte**

Hier sind are a few more holidays which you might experience during your visit.
- ❏ **das Neujahr** *(noy-yar)* . . . . New Year's
- ❏ **der Heiligabend** *(hi-leeg-ah-bent)* . . . . Christmas Eve
- ❏ **erster Weihnachtstag** *(vy-nahHts-tahk)* . . . . Christmas Day
- ❏ **das Ostern** *(oh-stairn)* . . . . Easter

Das Telefon
(tay-lay-fohn)
telephone

Was ist different about **das Telefon in** *(doych-lahnt)* **Deutschland?** Well, **Sie** never notice such things until

Sie want to use them. *(tay-lay-foh-nuh)* **Telefone** allow you to call *(froyn-duh)* **Freunde,** reserve *(tay-ah-tair-kar-ten)* **Theaterkarten,**
telephones   friends   theater tickets

(kohn-tsairt-kar-ten) *(bah-let-kar-ten)* *(moo-zay-oom)*
Konzertkarten, Balletkarten, make emergency calls, check on the hours of a **Museum,** rent

(ow-toh) *(mah-Hen)*
ein Auto und all those other **Dinge** which **wir machen** on a daily basis. It also gives you a
do

certain amount of freedom when **Sie können** your own calls *(mah-Hen)* **machen.**
make

(tay-lay-foh-nuh)
Telefone can usually be found everywhere:

in the **Post,** on the street, in cafes, at the
post office
(bahn-hohf)
Bahnhof and in the lobby of your **Hotel.**

The instructions can look complicated,

but remember, **Sie** should be able to

recognize some of these **Wörter** already.

(tay-lay-fohn-kar-tuh)
Most **Telefone** use **eine Telefonkarte.**
telephone card
(kuh-nen)
Sie können buy these **Telefonkarten** at

stores as well as at the **Post und** *(ahm)* **am**
at the
(bahn-hohf)
Bahnhof. Ready? Well, before you turn
train station

the page it would be a good idea to go back

und review all your numbers one more time.

To dial from the United States to most other countries **Sie** need that country's international

area code. Your *(tay-lay-fohn-booH)* **Telefonbuch** at home should have a listing of international area codes.
telephone book

Hier sind some very useful words built around the word „**Telefon**".
- [ ] **das Telefonbuch** *(tay-lay-fohn-booH)* . . . . telephone book
- [ ] **die Telefonzelle** *(tay-lay-fohn-tsel-luh)* . . . . telephone booth
- [ ] **das Telefongespräch** *(tay-lay-fohn-geh-shprayH)* . . . . telephone conversation
- [ ] **telefonieren** *(tay-lay-foh-neer-en)* . . . . to telephone

When **Sie** leave your contact numbers with friends, family **und** business colleagues, **Sie** should include your destination's country code **und** city code whenever possible . For example:

Country Codes		City Codes	
Germany	49	Berlin	30
		Frankfurt	69
Austria	43	Wien	1
		Innsbruck	512
Switzerland	41	Zürich	1

To call from one city to another city **in Deutschland, Sie** may need to go to **die Post oder** call

(tay-lay-foh-nee-stin) *(ear-em)* *(tay-lay-foh-nee-stin)*
die **Telefonistin** in Ihrem Hotel. Tell **die Telefonistin,**
operator   your

(nahH) *(shtoot-gart)* *(tay-lay-foh-neer-en)* *(mewn-shen)* *(tay-lay-foh-neer-en)*
„**Ich möchte nach Stuttgart telefonieren.**" oder „**Ich möchte nach München telefonieren.**"

Now you try it: _____
(I would like to telephone to . . . .)

When answering **das Telefon, Sie** pick up the receiver **und** say your **Name,**
(nah-muh)

(hah-loh) *(ah-pah-raht)*
Hallo, hier ist _____ **am Apparat.**
(Ihr Name)   on the phone

When saying goodbye, **Sie sagen, „Auf Wiederhören" oder „Tschüs"** Your turn —
(vee-dair-hur-en) *(choos)*
hear from you again   goodbye

_____
(Hello, here is . . . . on the phone.)

_____   _____
(goodbye)   (hear from you again)

Do not forget that **Sie können fragen** . . .
(frah-gen)
can

(vee-feel) *(tay-lay-fohn-geh-shprayH)* *(fair-eye-neeg-ten)* *(shtah-ten)*
Wieviel kostet ein Telefongespräch nach den Vereinigten Staaten? _____
U.S.A.

(kah-nah-dah)
Wieviel kostet ein Telefongespräch nach Kanada? _____

Hier sind some emergency telephone numbers.
- ❑ **die Polizei** *(poh-lih-tsy)* . . . . police   110 _____
- ❑ **die Feuerwehr** *(foy-air-vair)* . . . . fire department 112 _____
- ❑ **der Rettungsdienst** *(ret-toongs-deenst)* . . . . rescue service 112 _____
- ❑ **die Auskunft** *(ows-koonft)* . . . . information   11833 _____

Hier sind some sample sentences *(fewr)* **für das Telefon.** Write them in the blanks **unten.**

(murk-tuh)   *(my-ah-mee)* *(ahn-roo-fen)*
Ich möchte in Miami anrufen. _____
                           to call

(looft-hahn-zah)   *(ahn-roo-fen)*
Ich möchte Lufthansa in Frankfurt anrufen. _____

(eye-nen) *(arts-t)*
Ich möchte einen Arzt anrufen. _____
                  doctor

(my-nuh) *(noo-mair)*
Meine Nummer ist 67-59-48. _____
my

(vahs) *(ear-uh)* *(tay-lay-fohn-noo-mair)*
Was ist Ihre Telefonnummer? _____
what   your

(vahs)   *(hoh-tel-tay-lay-fohn-noo-mair)*
Was ist die Hoteltelefonnummer? _____

Christina: **Hallo, hier ist Christina** *(fah-bair)* **Faber. Ich möchte mit Frau** *(bres-lair)* **Bresler sprechen.**

_____

Sekretärin: **Einen** *(ow-gen-bleek)* **Augenblick.**   *(toot)* **Es tut mir** *(light)* **leid.**   **Es ist** *(beh-zets-t)* **besetzt.**
        one   moment   I'm sorry   busy, occupied

_____

Christina: *(vee-dair-hoh-len)* **Wiederholen Sie das bitte.**   **Sprechen Sie bitte** *(lahng-zah-mair)* **langsamer.**
        repeat   speak   more slowly

_____

Sekretärin: *(toot)* **Es tut mir** *(light)* **leid.**   **Es ist** *(beh-zets-t)* **besetzt.**

_____

Christina: **Ah. Danke.**   *(owf)* **Auf** *(vee-dair-hur-en)* **Wiederhören.**

_____

Sie sind nun ready to use any **Telefon in Deutschland.** Just take it *(lahng-zahm)* **langsam und** speak clearly.
                                slowly

Hier sind countries **Sie** may wish to call.

- ☐ **das Australien** *(ow-strah-lee-en)* .... Australia   _____
- ☐ **das Österreich** *(uh-stair-rike)* .... Austria   _____
- ☐ **das Belgien** *(bel-gee-en)* .... Belgium   _____
- ☐ **das Kanada** *(kah-nah-dah)* .... Canada

An excellent means of transportation **ist die U-Bahn** *(oo-bahn)*. **Die großen** *(groh-sen)* **Städte** *(shtay-tuh)* **haben eine**
large   cities

U-Bahn. Die kleineren *(kly-nair-en)* **Städte** *(shtay-tuh)* **haben eine Straßenbahn.** *(shtrah-sen-bahn)* **Both die U-Bahn und die**
smaller   streetcar

Straßenbahn (S-Bahn) sind einfach *(ein-fahH)* **und** quick ways to travel. Plus there is always the **Bus.** *(boos)*

die U-Bahn *(oo-bahn)*

subway

die Straßenbahn *(shtrah-sen-bahn)*

streetcar

die U-Bahnhaltestelle *(oo-bahn-hahl-tuh-shtel-luh)*

subway   stop

die Straßenbahnhaltestelle *(shtrah-sen-bahn-hahl-tuh-shtel-luh)*

streetcar   stop

die Bushaltestelle *(boos-hahl-tuh-shtel-luh)*

bus   stop

Maps displaying the various **Linien** *(lee-nee-en)* **und Haltestellen** *(hahl-tuh-shtel-len)* **sind** generally posted outside every
lines   stops

Eingang *(ein-gahng)* **für die U-Bahn.** Most **Stadtkarten** *(shtaht-kar-ten)* also have an **U-Bahn** map. **Die Linien** *(lee-nee-en)* **sind**
entrance   city maps   lines

color-coded to facilitate reading just like your example on the next page. If **Sie umsteigen** *(oom-shty-gen)*
transfer

müssen, *(mew-sen)* look for **die Verbindungen** *(fair-bin-doong-en)* clearly marked at each station.
must   connections, transfers

❑   **das England** *(eng-lahnt)* . . . . England   _____
❑   **das Spanien** *(shpah-nee-en)* . . . . Spain   _____
❑   **das Irland** *(ear-lahnt)* . . . . Ireland   _____
❑   **das Israel** *(eez-rah-el)* . . . . Israel   _____
❑   **das Italien** *(ee-tah-lee-en)* . . . . Italy

Other than having foreign words, **die deutsche U-Bahn** functions just like **in London oder in New York.** Locate your destination, select the correct line on your practice **U-Bahn und** hop on board.

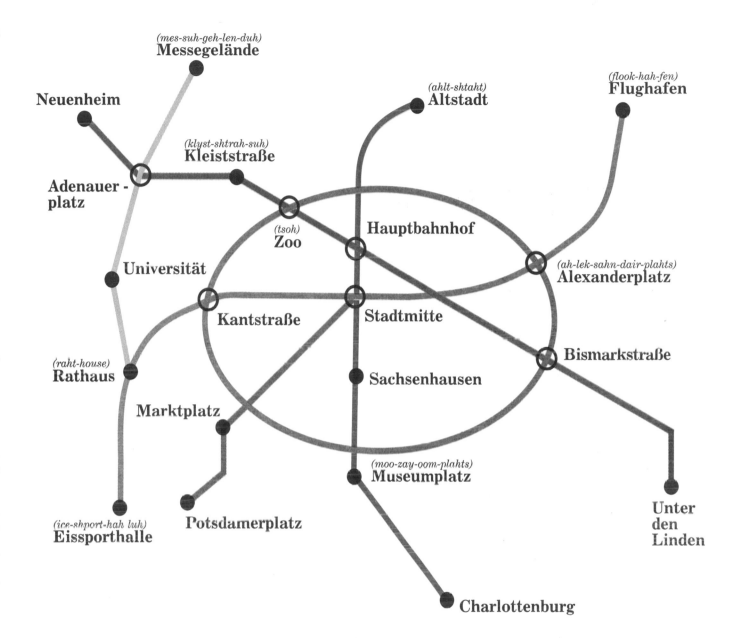

Say these questions aloud many times and don't forget you need **eine Karte für die U-Bahn.**

Wo ist die U-Bahnhaltestelle? *(oo-bahn-hahl-tuh-shtel-luh)*

Wo ist die Straßenbahnhaltestelle? *(shtrah-sen-bahn-hahl-tuh-shtel-luh)*

Wo ist die Bushaltestelle? *(boos-hahl-tuh-shtel-luh)*

- ❏ **das Frankreich** *(frahnk-rike)* .... France _____
- ❏ **das Holland** *(hohl-lahnt)* .... Holland _____
- ❏ **das Südafrika** *(zewt-ah-frih-kah)* .... South Africa _____
- ❏ **die Schweiz** *(shvites)* .... Switzerland _____
- ❏ **die Vereinigten Staaten** *(fair-eye-neeg-ten)(shtah-len)* United States _____

Practice the following basic **Fragen** out loud **und** **dann** *(dahn)* write them in the blanks below.
then

1. **Wie** *(vee)* **oft** **fährt** *(fairt)* **die U-Bahn** **zur** *(tsoor)* **Stadtmitte?** *(shtaht-mit-tuh)* _____
   how   often   travels   to the

   Wie oft fährt die Straßenbahn **zur** *(tsoor)* **Stadtmitte?** _____

   Wie oft fährt der **Bus** *(boos)* **zum** *(tsoom)* **Flughafen?** *(flook-hah-fen)* _____

2. **Wann** *(vahn)* **fährt** *(fairt)* **die U-Bahn** **ab?** *(ahp)* _____
   when   departs

   Wann *(vahn)* **fährt die Straßenbahn ab?** _____

   Wann fährt der **Bus** *(boos)* **ab?** _____

3. **Wieviel** *(vee-feel)* **kostet** *(koh-stet)* **eine** **U-Bahnkarte?** *(oo-bahn-kar-tuh)* _____

   Wieviel kostet eine Straßenbahnkarte? _____

   Wieviel kostet eine Buskarte? _____

4. **Wo** *(voh)* **ist die** **U-Bahnhaltestelle?** *(oo-bahn-hahl-tuh-shtel-luh)* _____

   Wo ist die Straßenbahnhaltestelle? _____

   Wo ist die Bushaltestelle? _____

Let's change directions **und** learn **drei** new verbs. **Sie** know the basic "plug-in" formula, so

write out your own sentences using these new verbs.

(vah-shen)
waschen _____
to wash

(fair-lear-en)
verlieren _____
to lose

(dow-airt)
es dauert _____
it lasts, it takes

Hier sind a few more holidays to keep in mind.

- ❏ **der Tag der Arbeit** *(tahk)(dair)(ar-bite)* . . . . Labor Day (May 1)
- ❏ **der Silvester** *(sil-ves-tair)* . . . . New Year's Eve
- ❏ **zweiter Weihnachtstag** *(tsvy-tair)(vy-nahHts-tahk)* . . . . Dec. 26
- ❏ **das Allerheiligen** *(ahl-lair-hi-lee-gen)* . . . . All Saints Day (Nov. 1)

23

Verkaufen und Kaufen
(fair-kow-fen) selling   *(kow-fen)* buying

Shopping abroad is exciting. The simple everyday task of buying **einen Liter Milch oder einen** *(lee-tair)* liter *(milsh)* milk

Apfel becomes a challenge that **Sie** should **nun** be able to meet quickly **und** easily. Of course, **Sie** *(ahp-fel)* apple

will purchase **Andenken, Briefmarken und Postkarten,** but do not forget those many other *(ahn-denk-en)* souvenirs *(breef-mar-ken)*

items ranging from shoelaces to aspirin that **Sie** might need unexpectedly. Locate your store,

draw a line to it **und,** as always, write your new words in the blanks provided.

das Kaufhaus _____
(kowf-house) department store

das Kino _____
(kee-noh) cinema

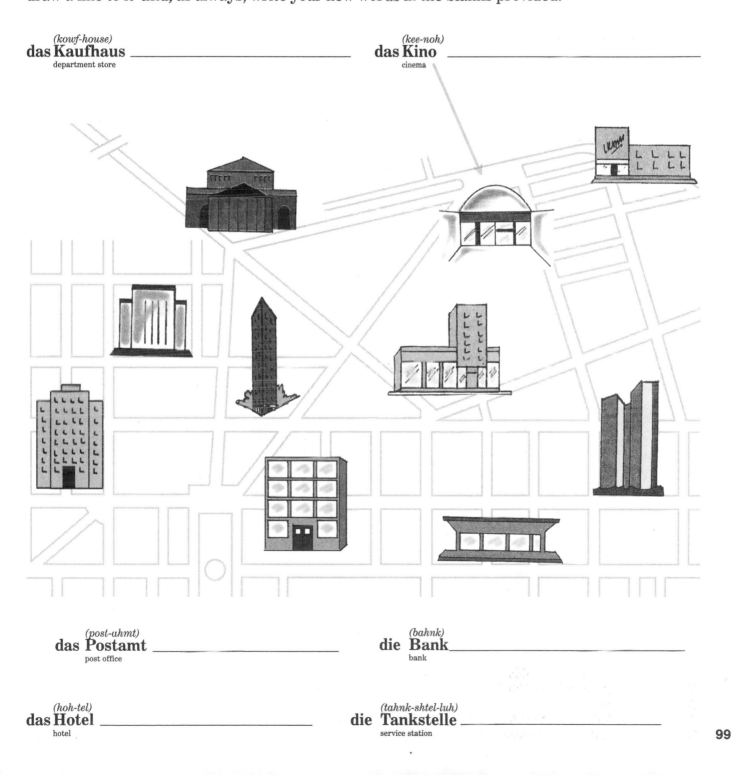

das Postamt _____
(post-ahmt) post office

die Bank _____
(bahnk) bank

das Hotel _____
(hoh-tel) hotel

die Tankstelle _____
(tahnk-shtel-luh) service station

(mets-gair-eye)
die Metzgerei
butcher shop

(booH-hahnt-loong)
die Buchhandlung
bookstore

_____ _____

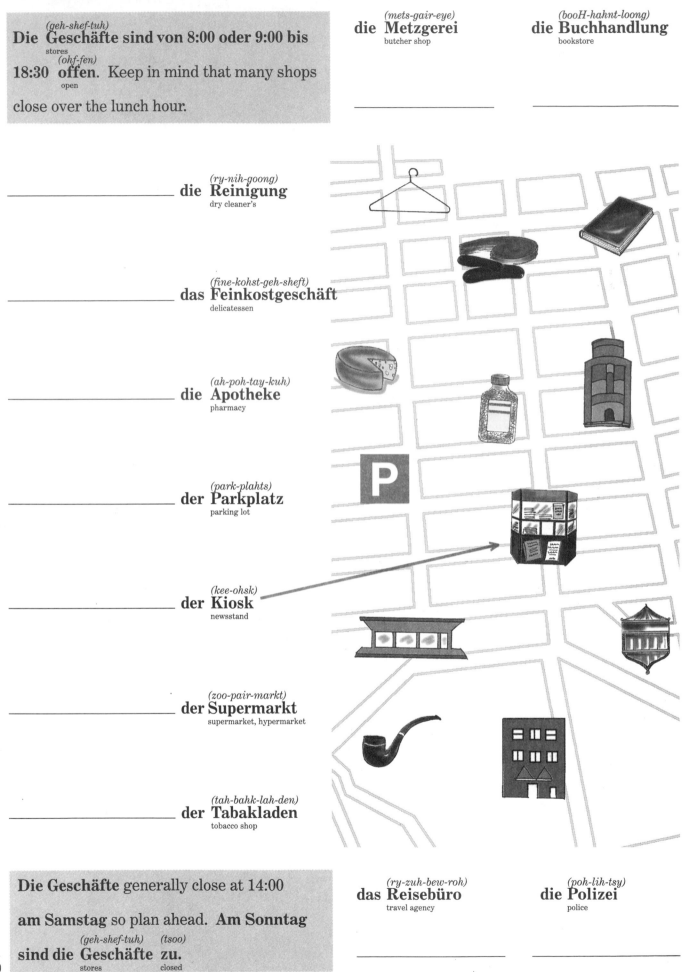

(ry-nih-goong)
_____ **die Reinigung**
dry cleaner's

(fine-kohst-geh-sheft)
_____ **das Feinkostgeschäft**
delicatessen

(ah-poh-tay-kuh)
_____ **die Apotheke**
pharmacy

(park-plahts)
_____ **der Parkplatz**
parking lot

(kee-ohsk)
_____ **der Kiosk**
newsstand

(zoo-pair-markt)
_____ **der Supermarkt**
supermarket, hypermarket

(tah-bahk-lah-den)
_____ **der Tabakladen**
tobacco shop

(ry-zuh-bew-roh)
das Reisebüro
travel agency

(poh-lih-tsy)
die Polizei
police

_____ _____

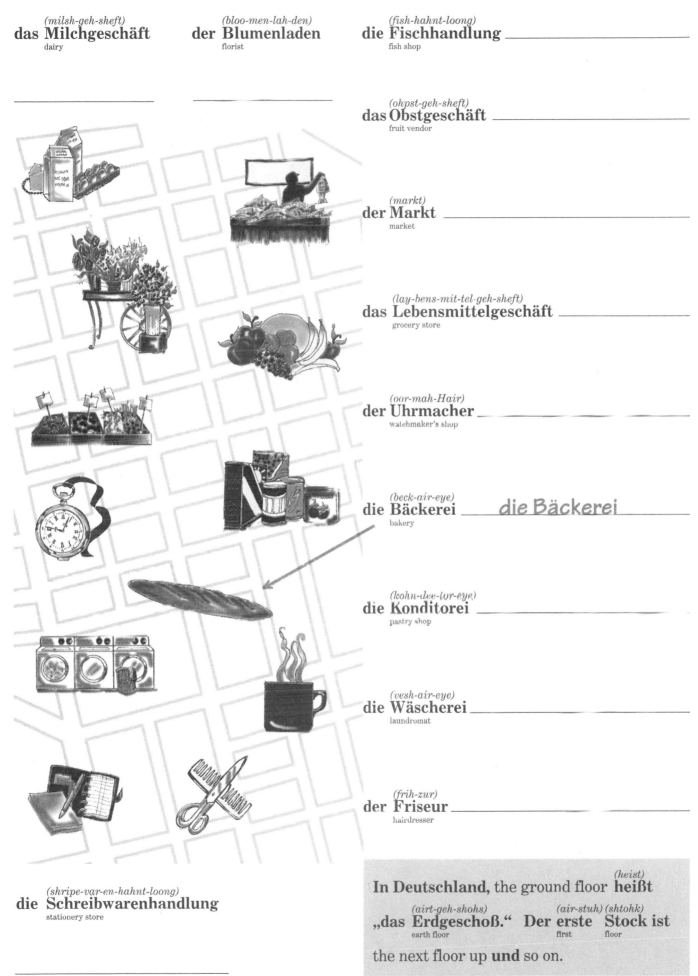

(milsh-geh-sheft)
das Milchgeschäft
dairy

(bloo-men-lah-den)
der Blumenladen
florist

(fish-hahnt-loong)
die Fischhandlung _____

(ohpst-geh-sheft)
das Obstgeschäft _____
fruit vendor

(markt)
der Markt _____
market

(lay-bens-mit-tel-geh-sheft)
das Lebensmittelgeschäft _____
grocery store

(oor-mah-Hair)
der Uhrmacher _____
watchmaker's shop

(beck-air-eye)
die Bäckerei ___die Bäckerei___
bakery

(kohn-dee-tor-eye)
die Konditorei _____
pastry shop

(vesh-air-eye)
die Wäscherei _____
laundromat

(frih-zur)
der Friseur _____
hairdresser

(shripe-var-en-hahnt-loong)
die Schreibwarenhandlung
stationery store

In Deutschland, the ground floor *(heist)* **heißt**
„das Erdgeschoß.“ Der erste Stock ist
earth floor · first · floor
the next floor up **und** so on.

24

Das Kaufhaus
(kowf-house)
department store

At this point, **Sie** should just about be ready for **Ihre** **Reise** *(ear-uh) (ry-zuh)*. **Sie** have gone shopping for those

last-minute odds 'n ends. Most likely, the store directory at your local **Kaufhaus** *(kowf-house)* did not look
department store

like the one **unten**. **Sie** **wissen** *(viss-en)* know that „**Kind**" *(kint)* is German for "child" so if **Sie** **brauchen** *(brow-Hen)*

something for a child, **Sie** would probably look on **Stock zwei oder drei,** *(shtohk)* floor wouldn't you?

4. ■ STOCK	Bestecke Elektro-Artikel Glas Delikatessen	Haushaltswaren Hobby Küchenmöbel Lebensmittel	Schlüsselbar Keramik Porzellan Weine
3. ■ STOCK	Bücher Fernsehen Kindermöbel Kinderwagen	Spielwaren Musikinstrumente Rundfunk Schreibwaren	Tabakwaren Teeraum Zeitschriften Zeitungen
2. ■ STOCK	Alles für das Kind Damenbekleidung Betten Bettfedern	Herrenbekleidung Damenhüte Lampen Teppiche	Fundbüro Kundendienst Cafeteria Plastik
1. ■ STOCK	Autozubehör Damenwäsche Taschentücher	Badeartikel Schuhe Handarbeiten	Bettwäsche Sportartikel Reisebüro
E	Foto-Optik Herrenhüte Schirme Schmuck	Handschuhe Lederwaren Strümpfe Uhren	Herrenartikel Parfümerie Süßwaren Bilder

Let's start a checklist **für** **Ihre** **Reise** *(ear-uh)* your. Besides **Kleider,** *(kly-dair)* clothing **was** *(vahs)* **brauchen** *(brow-Hen)* **Sie?** As you learn

these **Wörter,** assemble these items **in einer** **Ecke** *(eck-uh)* corner of your **Haus.** Check **und** make sure that

they **sind** **sauber** *(zow-bair)* clean **und** ready **für** **Ihre** **Reise** *(ear-uh)*. Be sure to do the same **mit** with the rest of the

Dinge things that **Sie packen** *(pah-ken)*. On the next pages, match each item to its picture, draw a line to it and

write out the word many times. As **Sie** organize these things, check them off on this list. Do

not forget to take the next group of sticky labels and label these **Dinge heute.** *(hoy-tuh)* today

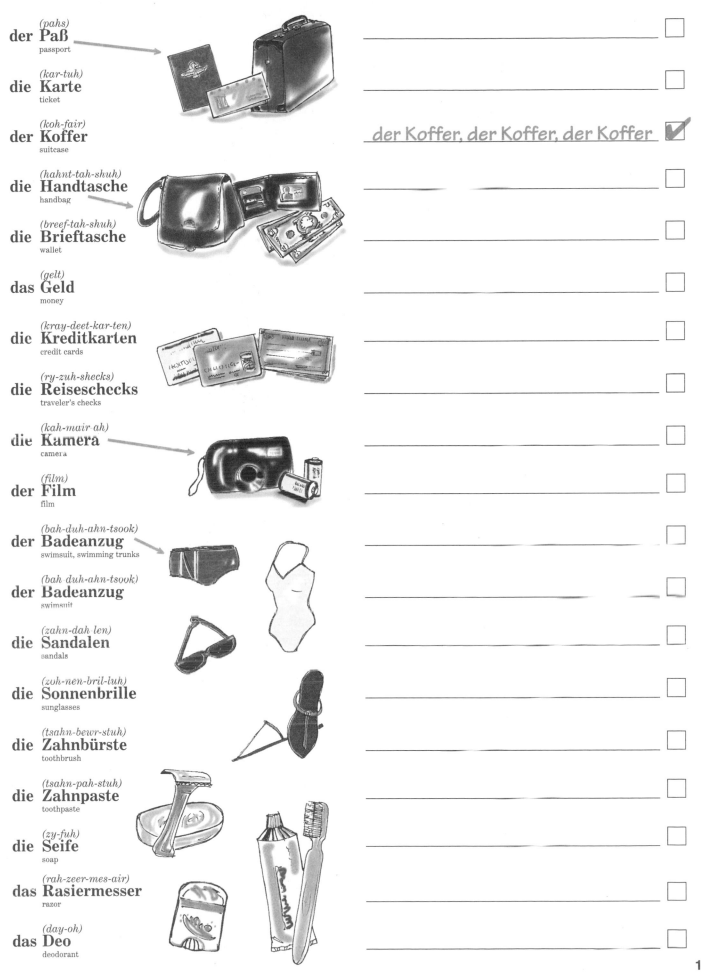

der Paß *(pahs)*
passport

die Karte *(kar-tuh)*
ticket

der Koffer *(koh-fair)*
suitcase

der Koffer, der Koffer, der Koffer ✓

die Handtasche *(hahnt-tah-shuh)*
handbag

die Brieftasche *(breef-tah-shuh)*
wallet

das Geld *(gelt)*
money

die Kreditkarten *(kray-deet-kar-ten)*
credit cards

die Reiseschecks *(ry-zuh-shecks)*
traveler's checks

die Kamera *(kah-mair-ah)*
camera

der Film *(film)*
film

der Badeanzug *(bah-duh-ahn-tsook)*
swimsuit, swimming trunks

der Badeanzug *(bah-duh-ahn-tsook)*
swimsuit

die Sandalen *(zahn-dah-len)*
sandals

die Sonnenbrille *(zoh-nen-bril-luh)*
sunglasses

die Zahnbürste *(tsahn-bewr-stuh)*
toothbrush

die Zahnpaste *(tsahn-pah-stuh)*
toothpaste

die Seife *(zy-fuh)*
soap

das Rasiermesser *(rah-zeer-mes-air)*
razor

das Deo *(day-oh)*
deodorant

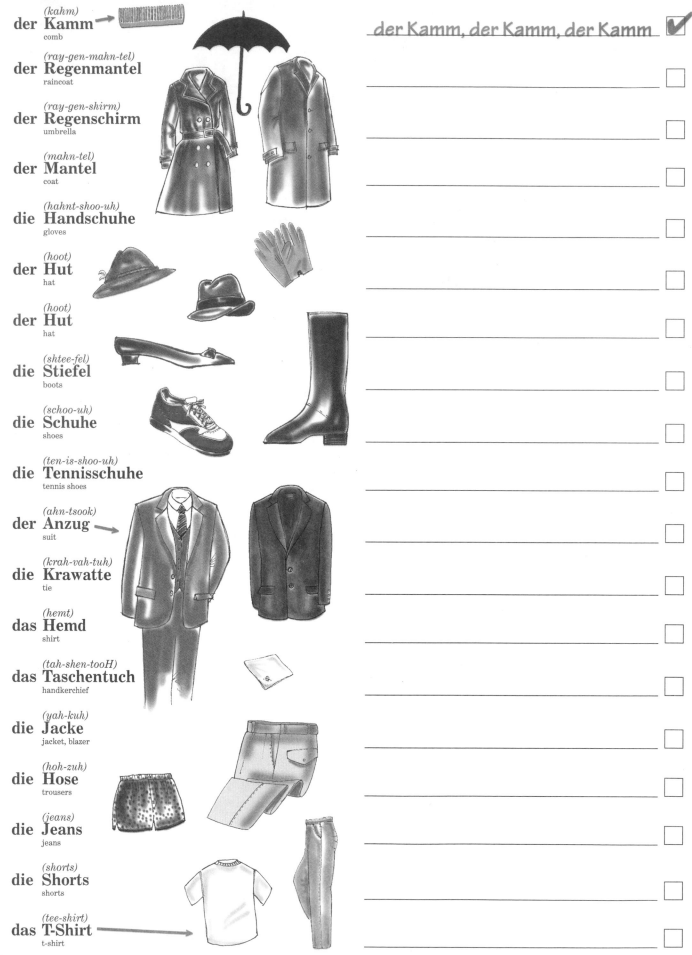

der **Kamm**
(kahm)
comb

der Kamm, der Kamm, der Kamm ✔

der **Regenmantel**
(ray-gen-mahn-tel)
raincoat

der **Regenschirm**
(ray-gen-shirm)
umbrella

der **Mantel**
(mahn-tel)
coat

die **Handschuhe**
(hahnt-shoo-uh)
gloves

der **Hut**
(hoot)
hat

der **Hut**
(hoot)
hat

die **Stiefel**
(shtee-fel)
boots

die **Schuhe**
(schoo-uh)
shoes

die **Tennisschuhe**
(ten-is-shoo-uh)
tennis shoes

der **Anzug**
(ahn-tsook)
suit

die **Krawatte**
(krah-vah-tuh)
tie

das **Hemd**
(hemt)
shirt

das **Taschentuch**
(tah-shen-tooH)
handkerchief

die **Jacke**
(yah-kuh)
jacket, blazer

die **Hose**
(hoh-zuh)
trousers

die **Jeans**
(jeans)
jeans

die **Shorts**
(shorts)
shorts

das **T-Shirt**
(tee-shirt)
t-shirt

die Unterhose *(oon-tair-hoh-zuh)*
underpants

☐

das Unterhemd *(oon-tair-hemt)*
undershirt →

☐

das Kleid *(klite)*
dress

☐

die Bluse *(bloo-zuh)*
blouse

☐

der Rock *(rohk)*
skirt

der Rock, der Rock, der Rock ✔

der Pulli *(poo-lee)*
sweater →

☐

der Unterrock *(oon-tair-rohk)*
slip

☐

der BH *(bay-hah)*
bra

☐

die Unterhose *(oon-tair-hoh-zuh)*
underpants

☐

die Socken *(zoh-ken)*
socks

☐

die Strumpfhose *(shtroomf-hoh-zuh)*
pantyhose

☐

der Schlafanzug *(shlahf-ahn-tsook)*
pajamas

☐

das Nachthemd *(nahHt-hemt)*
nightshirt

☐

der Bademantel *(bah-duh-mahn-tel)*
bathrobe

☐

die Hausschuhe *(house-shoo-uh)*
slippers

☐

From now on, **Sie haben „ Seife"** *(zy-fuh)* **und nicht** "soap." Having assembled these **Dinge, Sie**

sind ready **reisen.** Let's add these important shopping phrases to your basic repertoire.
   to travel

Welche Größe? *(vel-chuh) (gruh-suh)*_____
which   size

Es paßt. *(pahst)*_____
it   fits

Es paßt nicht. *(pahst)*_____
it   does not fit

105

Treat yourself to a final review. **Sie wissen die Namen für die deutschen Geschäfte,** so let's
<small>*(viss-en)*</small> / <small>know</small>

practice shopping. Just remember your key question **Wörter** that you learned in Step 2.

Whether **Sie** need to buy **einen Hut oder ein Buch** the necessary **Wörter sind** the same.
<small>*(hoot)*</small>

1. First step — **Wo?**
    <small>*(voh)*</small>

Wo ist die Bank?
<small>*(bahnk)*</small>

Wo ist das Kino?
<small>*(kee-noh)*</small>

Wo ist der Kiosk?
<small>*(kee-ohsk)*</small>

_____
(Where is the department store?)

_____
(Where is the grocery store?)

_____
(Where is the market?)

2. Second step — tell them what **Sie** are looking for, need **oder möchten!**

Ich brauche . . .
<small>*(brow-Huh)*</small>
<small>need</small>

Ich möchte . . .
<small>*(murk-tuh)*</small>
<small>would like</small>

Haben Sie . . . ?
<small>*(hah-ben)*</small>
<small>do you have</small>

_____
(Do you have postcards?)

_____
(I would like four stamps.)

_____
(I need toothpaste.)

_____
(I would like to buy film.)

_____
(Do you have coffee?)

Go through the glossary at the end of this **Buch und** select **zwanzig Wörter.** (tsvahn-tsig) Drill the above

patterns **mit** **diesen** (dee-zen) **zwanzig Wörtern.** Don't cheat. Drill them **heute. Nun,** take **zwanzig**

mehr Wörter von (mair) **Ihrem** (ear-em) **Wörterbuch** (vur-tair-booH) **und** do the same.
your · dictionary
these

3. Third step — find out **wieviel es kostet.** (vee-feel)

Wieviel kostet das? (vee-feel) (dahs)   **Wieviel kostet die Postkarte?** (koh-stet)   **Wieviel kostet das Bild?** (bilt)

_____

(How much does the toothpaste cost?)

_____

(How much does the soap cost?)

_____

(How much does a cup of tea cost?)

4.   Fourth step — success! I found it!

Once **Sie finden** what **Sie** would like, **Sie sagen,** (zah-gen)
say

Ich möchte das bitte. _Ich möchte das bitte. Ich möchte das bitte._

or

Ich nehme das bitte. (nay-muh) _____
take

Oder if **Sie** would not like it, **Sie sagen,**

Ich möchte das nicht. (neeHt) _____

or

Ich nehme das nicht. (nay-muh) _____
do not take

Congratulations! You have finished. By now you should have stuck your labels, flashed your

cards, cut out your menu guide and packed your suitcases. You should be very pleased with your

accomplishment. You have learned what it sometimes takes others years to achieve and you

hopefully had fun doing it. **Gute Reise!** (goo-tuh) (ry-zuh)

Glossary

This glossary contains words used in this book only. It is not meant to be a dictionary. Consider purchasing a dictionary which best suits your needs - small for traveling, large for reference, or specialized for specific vocabulary needs.

A

Abend, der (ah-bent) . . . . evening
Abendessen, das (ah-bent-ess-en) . . . . dinner
abends (ah-bents) . . . . evenings, in the evening
abfahren (ahp-far-en) . . . . to depart, leave
Abfahrt, die (ahp-fahrt) . . . . departure
Abteil, das (ahp-tile) . . . . compartment
acht (ahHt) . . . . eight
achtzehn (ahHt-tsayn) . . . . eighteen
achtzig (ahHt-tsig) . . . . eighty
Adresse, die (ah-dres-suh) . . . . address
Akademie, die (ah-kah-deh-mee) . . . . academy
Akt, der (ahkt) . . . . act (of a play)
Akzent, der (ahk-tsent) . . . . parents
Alkohol, die (ahl-koh-hohl) . . . . alcohol
alle (ahl-luh) . . . . all, everyone
alles (ahl-les) . . . . everything
Alpen, die (ahl-pen) . . . . the Alps
Alphabet, das (ahl-fah-bate) . . . . alphabet
alt (ahlt) . . . . old
am (= an dem) . . . . at the, on the
Amerika, das (ah-mair-ih-kah) . . . . America
Amerikaner, der (ah-mair-ih-kahn-air) . . American
an (ahn) . . . . on, upon (vertical surfaces), at
Andenken, das (ahn-denk-en) . . . . souvenir
ankommen (ahn-koh-men) . . . . to arrive
Ankunft, die (ahn-koonft) . . . . arrival
Anruf, der (ahn-roof) . . . . call, telephone call
anrufen (ahn-roo-fen) . . . . to call
Anschrift, die (ahn-shrift) . . . . address
Antwort, die (ahnt-vort) . . . . answer
Anzug, der (ahn-tsook) . . . . suit
Apfel, der (ahp-fel) . . . . apple
Apotheke, die (ah-poh-tay-kuh) . . . . pharmacy
Apparat, der (ah-pah-raht) . . . . telephone, receiver
Appetit, der (ah-peh-teet) . . . . appetite
April, der (ah-pril) . . . . April
arm (arm) . . . . poor
Arzt, der (arts-t) . . . . physician
auch (owH) . . . . also
auf (owf) . . . . . on top of (horizontal surfaces), open
auf Deutsch (owf)(doych) . . . . in German
Auf Wiederhören! (owf)(vee-dair-hur-en) . . . .
. . . . Hear from you again!
Auf Wiedersehen! (owf)(vee-dair-zay-en) . . . .
. . . . See you again!, goodbye
Aufschnitt, der (owf-shnit) . . . . cold cuts
aufschreiben (owf-shry-ben) . . . . to write out
Augenblick, der (ow-gen-bleek) . . . . moment
August, der (ow-goost) . . . . August
aus (ows) . . . . out of, from
Ausfahrt, die (ows-fahrt) . . . . exit (for vehicles)
Ausgang, der (ows-gahng) . . . . exit (for people)
Auskunft, die (ows-koonft) . . . . information
Ausland, das (ows-lahnt) . . . . abroad

Australien, das (ow-shtrah-lee-en) . . . . . . Australia
Auto, das (ow-toh) (die Autos) . . . . car
Autobahn, die (ow-toh-bahn) . . . . freeway
Autor, der (ow-tor) . . . . author

B

BH, der (bay-hah) . . . . bra
Bäckerei, die (beck-air-eye) . . . . bakery
Bad, das (baht) . . . . bath
Badeanzug, der (bah-duh-ahn-tsook) . bathing suit
Bademantel, der (bah-duh-mahn-tel) . . . . bathrobe
baden (bah-den) . . . . to bathe
Badezimmer, das (bah-duh-tsih-mair) . . bathroom
Bahnhof, der (bahn-hohf) . . . . train station
Bahnsteig, der (bahn-shtaig) . . . . railway platform
Ball, der (bahl) . . . . ball
Ballett, das (bah-let) . . . . ballet
Ballettkarte, die (bah-let-kar-tuh) . . . . ballet ticket
Banane, die (bah-nah-nuh) . . . . banana
Bank, die (bahnk) . . . . bank
Bedienung, die (beh-dee-noong) . . . . service charge
Beefsteak, das (beef-steak) . . . . beefsteak
Belgien, das (bel-gee-en) . . . . Belgium
besetzt (beh-zets-t) . . . . occupied
besser (bes-air) . . . . better
bestellen (beh-shtel-len) . . . . to order
Bett, das (bet) . . . . bed
Bettdecke, die (bet-deck-uh) . . . blanket, bedspread
bezahlen (beh-tsah-len) . . . . to pay
Bier, das (beer) . . . . beer
Bierstein, der (beer-stein) . . . . beer mug
Bild, das (bilt) . . . . picture
billig (bil-lig) . . . . cheap
bin (bin) . . . . (I) am
bitte (bit-tuh) . . . . please, you're welcome
bitte schön (bit-tuh)(shuhn) . . . you're very welcome
blau (blau) . . . . blue
bleiben (bly-ben) . . . . to remain, stay
Bleistift, der (bly-shtift) . . . . pencil
Blume, die (bloo-muh) . . . . flower
Blumenladen, der (bloo-men-lah-den) . . flower shop
Bluse, die (bloo-zuh) . . . . blouse
Boot, das (boht) . . . . boat
brauchen (brow-Hen) . . . . to need
braun (brown) . . . . brown
Brief, der (breef) . . . . letter
Briefkasten, der (breef-kah-sten) . . . . mailbox
Briefmarke, die (breef-mar-kuh) . . . . stamp
Brieftasche, die (breef-tah-shuh) . . . . wallet
Brille, die (bril-luh) . . . . eyeglasses
bringen (bring-en) . . . . to bring
Brot, das (broht) . . . . bread
Brötchen, das (bruht-chen) . . . . roll
Bruder, der (broo-dair) . . . . brother
Buch, das (booH) . . . . book
Buchhandlung, die (booH-hahnt-loong) . bookstore

bunt *(boont)* . . . . multi-colored
Büro, das *(bew-roh)* . . . . office, study
Bus, der *(boos)* . . . . bus
Bushaltestelle, die *(boos-hahl-tuh-shtel-luh)* . . . . .
. . . . bus stop
Butter, die *(boo-tair)* . . . . butter

C

Café, das *(kah-fay)* . . . . café
Celsius, das *(sel-see-oos)* . . . . centigrade
Champagner, der *(shahm-pahn-yair)* . . . champagne
Chemie, die *(shay-mee)* . . . . chemistry
Chile, das *(she-lay)* . . . . Chile
China, das *(she-nah)* . . . . China
chinesisch *(she-nay-zish)* . . . . Chinese
Chor, der *(kor)* . . . . choir
christlich *(krist-leeH)* . . . . Christian
Computer, der *(kohm-pyoo-tair)* . . . . computer

D

DM . . . . abbrev. for German mark
Dame, die *(dah-muh)* . . . . lady
Dänemark, das *(day-nuh-mark)* . . . . Denmark
Dänisch, das *(day-nish)* . . . . Danish
danke *(dahn-kuh)* . . . . thank you
danke schön *(dahn-kuh)(shuhn)* . . . .
. . . . thank you very much
dann *(dahn)* . . . . then
das *(duhs)* . . . . the, that
dauert *(dow airt)* . . . . (it) lasts, takes
dem *(dehm)* . . . . the
den *(dehn)* . . . . the
Deo, das *(day-oh)* . . . . deodorant
der *(dair)* . . . . the, of the
des *(des)* . . . . the, of the
Deutsch, das *(doych)* . . . . German
deutsch *(doych)* . . . . German
deutsche *(doy-chuh)* . . . . German
Deutschen, die *(doy-chen)* . . . . . . German people
Deutschland, das *(doych-luhnt)* . . . . Germany
Dezember, der *(day-tsem-bair)* . . . . December
die *(dee)* . . . . the
Dienstag, der *(deens-tahk)* . . . . Tuesday
diesen *(dee-zen)* . . . . this, that, these
Ding, das *(ding)* . . . . thing
Doktor, der *(dohk-tor)* . . . . doctor (title)
Donnerstag, der *(doh-nairs-tahk)* . . . . . Thursday
dort *(dort)* . . . . there
drei *(dry)* . . . . three
dreißig *(dry-sig)* . . . . thirty
dreizehn *(dry-tsayn)* . . . . thirteen
Drogerie, die *(droh-geh-ree)* . . . . drugstore
drücken *(drew-ken)* . . . . to push (doors)
du *(doo)* . . . . you (informal, singular)
Durst, der *(doorst)* . . . . thirst
Dusche, die *(doosh-uh)* . . . . shower

E

Ecke, die *(eck-uh)* . . . . corner
Ei, das *(eye)* . . . . egg
Eierspeisen, die *(eye-air-shpy-zen)* . . . . egg dishes
Eilzüge, die *(ile-tsue-guh)* . . . . . medium-fast trains
ein *(ein)* . . . . a
ein bißchen *(ein)(bis-Hen)* . . . . a little

ein Paar *(ein)(par)* . . . . a pair, a couple
eine *(eye-nuh)* . . . . a
einem *(eye-nem)* . . . . a, to a
einen *(eye-nen)* . . . . a
einer *(eye-nair)* . . . . a, of a
eines *(eye-nes)* . . . . a, of a
einfach *(ein-fahH)* . . . . one-way, simple
Einfahrt, die *(ein-fahrt)* . . . entrance (for vehicles)
Eingang, der *(ein-gahng)* . . . entrance (for people)
eins *(eins)* . . . . one
Eis, das *(ice)* . . . . ice cream
Elefant, der *(ay-lay-fahnt)* . . . . elephant
elf *(elf)* . . . . eleven
Eltern, die *(el-tairn)* . . . . parents
England, das *(eng-lahnt)* . . . . England
Engländer, der *(eng-len-dair)* . . . . . English (male)
Englisch, das *(eng-lish)* . . . . English
Entschuldigung *(ent-shool-dee-goong)* . . excuse me
er *(air)* . . . . he
Erdgeschoß, das *(airt-geh-shohs)* . . . . ground floor
erste *(air-stuh)* . . . . first
es *(es)* . . . . it
es gibt *(es)(gipt)* . . . . there is, there are
es tut mir leid *(es)(toot)(mir)(light)* . . . I am sorry
essen *(ess-en)* . . . . to eat
Essen, das *(ess-en)* . . . . meal
Eßzimmer, das *(ess-tsih-mair)* . . . . . dining room
Europa, das *(oy-roh-pah)* . . . . Europe
europäisch *(oy-roh-pay-ish)* . . . . European
evangelisch *(ay-vahn-gay-lish)* . . . . Protestant

F

fahren *(fah-ren)* . . . . to go, drive, travel
Fahrenheit, die *(fah-ren-hite)* . . . . Fahrenheit
Fahrkarte, die *(far-kar-tuh)* . . . . ticket
Fahrplan, der *(far-plahn)* . . . . timetable
Fahrrad, das *(far-raht)* . . . . bicycle
Familie, die *(fah-mee-lee-uh)* . . . . family
fantastisch *(fahn-tahs-tish)* . . . . fantastic
Farbe, die *(far-buh)* . . . . color
Fax, das *(fahks)* . . . . fax
Februar, der *(fay-broo-ar)* . . . . February
Feinkostgeschäft, das *(fine-kohst-geh-sheft)* . . . . . .
. . . . delicatessen
Fenster, das *(fehn-stair)* . . . . window
Ferngespräch, das *(fairn-geh-shprayH)* . . . .
. . . . long-distance telephone call
Fernseher, der *(fairn-zay-air)* . . . . . . television set
Feuerwehr, die *(foy-air-vair)* . . . . . fire department
Film, der *(film)* . . . . film
finden *(fin-den)* . . . . to find
Finger, der *(fing-air)* . . . . finger
Fisch, der *(fish)* . . . . fish
Fischgerichte, die *(fish-geh-reeH-tuh)* . . fish entrees
Fischhandlung, die *(fish-hahnt-loong)* . . . fish store
Flasche, die *(flah-shuh)* . . . . bottle
Fleisch, das *(fly-sh)* . . . . meat
fliegen *(flee-gen)* . . . . to fly
Flug, der *(flook)* . . . . flight
Flughafen, der *(flook-hah-fen)* . . . . airport
Flugkarte, die *(flook-kar-tuh)* . . . . airplane ticket
Flugzeug, das *(flook-tsoyk)* . . . . airplane
Frage, die *(frah-guh)* . . . . question
fragen *(frah-gen)* . . . . to ask **109**

Frankreich, das *(frahnk-rike)* . . . . France
Französisch, das *(frahn-tsuh-zish)* . . . . French
Frau, die *(frow)* . . . . woman, Mrs.
Fräulein, das *(froy-line)* . . . . young lady, Miss
frei *(fry)* . . . . free of charge, available
Freitag, der *(fry-tahk)* . . . . Friday
Freund, der *(froynt)* . . . . friend
Friseur, der *(frih-zur)* . . . . hairdresser
Frühling, der *(frew-ling)* . . . . spring
Frühstück, das *(frew-shtewk)* . . . . breakfast
Fundbüro, das *(foont-bew-roh)* . lost-and-found office
fünf *(fewnf)* . . . . five
fünfhundert *(fewnf-hoon-dairt)* . . . . . . five hundred
fünfzehn *(fewnf-tsayn)* . . . . fifteen
fünfzig *(fewnf-tsig)* . . . . fifty
für *(fewr)* . . . . for

G

Gabel, die *(gah-bel)* . . . . fork
Garage, die *(gah-rah-zhuh)* . . . . garage
Garten, der *(gar-ten)* . . . . garden, yard
Gasthaus, das *(gahst-house)* . . . . restaurant, inn
gebacken *(geh-bah-ken)* . . . . baked
geben *(gay-ben)* . . . . to give
Geben Sie mir . . . *(gay-ben)(zee)(mir)* . . give me . . !
gebraten *(geh-brah-ten)* . . . . roasted, fried
Geflügel, das *(geh-flew-gel)* . . . . poultry
gefüllt *(geh-fewlt)* . . . . stuffed
gegrillt *(geh-grilt)* . . . . grilled
gehen *(gay-en)* . . . . to go
geht *(gate)* . . . . goes
gekocht *(geh-kohHt)* . . . . cooked, boiled
gelb *(gelp)* . . . . yellow
Geld, das *(gelt)* . . . . money
Geldscheine, die *(gelt-shy-nuh)* . . . . bank notes
Geldstücke, die *(gelt-shtew-kuh)* . . . . coins
gemischt *(geh-misht)* . . . . mixed
Gemüse, das *(geh-mew-zuh)* . . . . vegetables
geradeaus *(geh-rah-duh-ows)* . . . . . . straight ahead
Geschäft, das *(geh-sheft)* . . . . store
Geschwindigkeitsbegrenzung, die *(geh-shvin-deeg-kites-beh-gren-tsoong)* . . . . speed limit
gesperrt *(geh-shpairt)* . . . . closed, blocked
Gespräch, das *(geh-shprayH)* . . . . conversation
gestern *(ges-tairn)* . . . . yesterday
gesund *(geh-zoont)* . . . . healthy
Getränke, die *(geh-trenk-uh)* . . . . beverages
Glas, das *(glahs)* . . . . glass
Gleis, das *(glice)* . . . . track
Glück, das *(glewk)* . . . . luck
Goethe *(guh-tuh)* . . . . 18ᵗʰ century writer
Grad, der *(grahd)* . . . . degree
grau *(grau)* . . . . gray
Grill- und Pfannengerichte, die *(gril-oont-fahn-en-geh-reeH-tuh)* . . . . grilled and fried entrees
groß *(grohs)* . . . . large
Größe, die *(gruh-suh)* . . . . size
Großmutter, die *(grohs-moo-tair)* . . . . . grandmother
Großvater, der *(grohs-vah-tair)* . . . . . . grandfather
grün *(grewn)* . . . . green
Gulasch, das *(goo-lahsh)* . . . . goulash
gut, gutes, gute *(goot)(goo-tes)(goo-tuh)* . . . . . . good
Gute Nacht *(goo-tuh)(nahHt)* . . . . good night
110 **Gute Reise!** *(goo-tuh)(ry-zuh)* . . . . Have a good trip!

Guten Abend *(goo-ten)(ah-bent)* . . . . . good evening
Guten Appetit *(goo-ten)(ah-peh-teet)* . . . .
. . . . enjoy your meal
Guten Morgen *(goo-ten)(mor-gen)* . . good morning
Guten Tag *(goo-ten)(tahk)* . . . . good day, hello

H

haben *(hah-ben)* . . . . to have
halb *(hahlp)* . . . . half
Halle, die *(hah-luh)* . . . . hall
Haltestelle, die *(hahl-tuh-shtel-luh)* . . . .
. . . . transportation stop
Handschuhe, die *(hahnt-shoo-uh)* . . . . gloves
Handtasche, die *(hahnt-tah-shuh)* . . . . purse
hat *(haht)* . . . . has
Haupteingang, der *(howpt-ein-gahng)* . . main entrance
Hauptgerichte, die *(howpt-geh-reeH-tuh)* . . . .
. . . . main meals, entrees
Haus, das *(house)* . . . . house
Hauschuhe, die *(house-shoo-uh)* . . . . slippers
Heiligabend, der *(hi-leeg-ah-bent)* . . Christmas Eve
heiß *(hice)* . . . . hot
heißen *(hi-sen)* . . . . to be called
Hemd, das *(hemt)* . . . . shirt
Herbst, der *(hairp-st)* . . . . fall
Herd, der *(hairt)* . . . . stove
Herr, der *(hair)* . . . . gentleman, Mr.
Herr Ober! *(hair)(oh-bair)* . . . . Waiter!
heute *(hoy-tuh)* . . . . today
hier *(here)* . . . . here
Hilfe! *(hil-fuh)* . . . . help!
hin und zurück *(hin)(oont)(tsoo-rewk)* . . there and back
hinter *(hin-tair)* . . . . behind
hoch *(hohH)* . . . . high
Holland, das *(hohl-lahnt)* . the Netherlands, Holland
Hose, die *(hoh-zuh)* . . . . trousers
Hotel, das *(hoh-tel)* . . . . hotel
Hotelzimmer, das *(hoh-tel-tsih-mair)* . . . . hotel room
Hund, der *(hoont)* . . . . dog
hundert *(hoon-dairt)* . . . . hundred
Hunger, der *(hoong-air)* . . . . hunger
Hut, der *(hoot)* . . . . hat

I

ich *(eeH)* I
Idee, die *(ee-day)* . . . . idea
Ihnen *(ee-nen)* . . . . to you
ihr *(ear)* . . . . you (informal, plural)
Ihr, Ihre, Ihrem *(ear)(ear-uh)(ear-em)* . . . . . . your
im *(= in dem)* . . . . in, in the
im Backteig *(im)(bahk-taig)* . . . . . . in batter, dough
in *(in)* . . . . in
Information, die *(in-for-mah-tsee-ohn)* . . information
Inland, das *(in-lahnt)* . . . . inland, domestic
Institut, das *(in-stee-toot)* . . . . institute
interessant *(in-tair-es-sahnt)* . . . . interesting
Irland, das *(ear-lahnt)* . . . . Ireland
Israel, das *(eez-rah-el)* . . . . Israel
ist *(ist)* . . . . is
Italien, das *(ee-tah-lee-en)* . . . . Italy
Italienisch, die *(ee-tah-lee-ay-nish)* . . Italian (language)

J

ja *(yah)* . . . . yes

Jacke, die *(yah-kuh)* . . . . jacket
Jahr, das *(yar)* . . . . year
Januar, der *(yah-noo-ar)* . . . . January
Japan, das *(yah-pahn)* . . . . Japan
Japanisch, das *(yah-pah-nish)* . . . . Japanese
Jeans, die *(jeans)* . . . . jeans
jetzt *(yets-t)* . . . . now
Journal, das *(zhoor-nahl)* . . . . . . journal, magazine
jüdisch *(yew-dish)* . . . . Jewish
Juli, der *(yoo-lee)* . . . . July
jung *(yoong)* . . . . young
Juni, der *(yoo-nee)* . . . . June

K

Kabine, die *(kah-bee-nuh)* . . . . booth
Kaffee, der *(kah-fay)* . . . . coffee
Kaffeehaus, das *(kah-fay-house)* . . . . . . coffee house
Kakao, der *(kah-kow)* . . . . hot chocolate
Kalender, der *(kah-len-dair)* . . . . calendar
kalt *(kahlt)* . . . . cold
Kamera, die *(kah-mair-uh)* . . . . camera
Kamm, der *(kahm)* . . . . comb
Kanada, das *(kah-nah-dah)* . . . . Canada
Kanadier, der *(kah-nah-dyair)* . . . Canadian (male)
kann *(kahn)* . . . . he, she, it can
Kännchen, das *(ken-chen)* . . . . pot
Karotten, die *(kah-roh-ten)* . . . . carrots
Karte, die *(kar-tuh)* . . . . card, ticket, map
Kartoffeln, die *(kar-toh-feln)* . . . . potatoes
Käse, der *(kay-zuh)* . . . . cheese
Kasse, die *(kah-suh)* . . . . cashier
katholisch *(kah-toh-lish)* . . . . Catholic
Katze, die *(kah-tsuh)* . . . . cat
Kaufhaus, das *(kowf-house)* . . . . . . department store
kaufen *(kow-fen)* . . . . to buy
kein *(kine)* . . . . no
Keller, der *(kel-air)* . . . . cellar
Kellner, der *(kel-nair)* . . . . waiter
Kellnerin, die *(kel-nair-in)* . . . . waitress
Kilometer, der *(kee-loh-may-tair)* . . . . . . kilometer
Kind, das *(kint)* . . . . child
Kino, das *(kee-noh)* . . . . movie theater
Kiosk, der *(kee-ohsk)* . . . . newsstand
Kirche, die *(kir-Huh)* . . . . church
Kleid, das *(klite)* . . . . dress,
Kleiderschrank, der *(kly-dair-shrahnk)* . . clothes closet
klein *(kline)* . . . . small
kochen *(koh-Hen)* . . . . to cook
Koffer, der *(koh-fair)* . . . . suitcase
kommen *(koh-men)* . . . . to come
kommt *(kohmt)* . . . . comes
Konditorei, die *(kohn-dee-tor-eye)* . pastry shop, café
können *(kuh-nen)* . . . . to be able to, can
Konversation, die *(kohn-vair-zah-tsee-ohn)* . . . .
. . . . conversation
Konzert, das *(kohn-tsairt)* . . . . concert
Konzertkarte, die *(kohn-tsairt-kar-tuh)* concert ticket
Kopfkissen, das *(kohpf-kiss-en)* . . . . pillow
kosten *(koh-sten)* . . . . to cost
kostet *(koh-stet)* . . . . costs
Kotelett, das *(koh-teh-let)* . . . . cutlet, chop
krank *(krahnk)* . . . . sick, ill
Krawatte, die *(krah-vah-tuh)* . . . . tie
Kreditkarten, die *(kray-deet-kar-ten)* . . . credit cards

Kreuzworträtsel, das *(kroits-vort-rate-sel)* . . . .
. . . . crossword puzzle
Küche, die *(kew-Huh)* . . . . kitchen
Kuchen, der *(koo-Hen)* . . . . cake, pastry
Kuckucksuhr, die *(koo-kooks-oor)* . . . . cuckoo clock
kühl *(kewl)* . . . . cool
Kühlschrank, der *(kewl-shrahnk)* . . . . . . refrigerator
Kuli, der *(koo-lee)* . . . . pen
kurz *(koorts)* . . . . short

L

Lamm, das *(lahm)* . . . . lamb
Lampe, die *(lahm-puh)* . . . . lamp
Land, das *(lahnt)* . . . . land, country
landen *(lahn-den)* . . . . to land
Landkarte, die *(lahnt-kar-tuh)* . . . . map
Landmarke, die *(lahnt-mar-kuh)* . . . . landmark
Landung, die *(lahn-doong)* . . . . landing
lang *(lahng)* . . . . long
langsam *(lahng-zahm)* . . . . slow
langsamer *(lahng-zah-mair)* . . . slower, more slowly
laut *(lout)* . . . . loud
Lebensmittelgeschäft, das *(lay-bens-mit-tel-geh-sheft)*
. . . . grocery store
lernen *(lair-nen)* . . . . to learn
lesen *(lay-zen)* . . . . to read
Licht, das *(leeHt)* . . . . light
Liegewagen, der *(lee-guh-vah-gen)* . . car with berths
Likör, der *(lee-kur)* . . . . liqueur
Limonade, die *(lee-moh-nah-duh)* . . . . . . lemonade
Linie, die *(lee-nee-uh)* . . . . line
links *(links)* . . . . left
Liter, der *(lee-tair)* . . . . liter
Löffel, der *(luh-fel)* . . . . spoon
Lokomotive, die *(loh-koh-moh-tee-vuh)* . . locomotive
los *(lohs)* . . . . wrong
Luftpost, die *(looft-post)* . . . . airmail
Luxemburg, das *(look-sem-boorg)* . . . . . Luxembourg

M

machen *(mah-Hen)* . . . . to make, do
Mai, der *(my)* . . . . May
man *(mahn)* . . . . one
Mann, der *(mahn)* . . . . man
Männer, die *(men-air)* . . . . men
Mantel, der *(mahn-tel)* . . . . coat
Mark, die *(mark)* . . . mark (unit of German currency)
Markt, der *(markt)* . . . . market
Marmelade, die *(mar-meh-lah-duh)* . jam, marmalade
März, der *(merts)* . . . . March
Mechaniker, der *(may-Hahn-ee-kair)* . . . . mechanic
mehr *(mair)* . . . . more
Meile, die *(my-luh)* . . . . mile
mein, meine *(mine)(my-nuh)* . . . . my
Menü, das *(men-ew)* . . . . menu
Messegelände, das *(mes-suh-geh-len-dah)* . fair grounds
Messer, das *(mes-air)* . . . . knife
Meter, der *(may-tair)* . . . . meter
Metzgerei, die *(mets-gair-eye)* . . . . butcher shop
mich *(meeH)* . . . . me
Mietwagen, der *(meet-vah-gen)* . . . . . rental car
Milch, die *(milsh)* . . . . milk
Milchgeschäft, das *(milsh-geh-sheft)* . . . . dairy   **111**

Mineralwasser, das *(mih-nair-ahl-vah-sair)* . . . . mineral water
Minute, die *(mee-noo-tuh)* . . . . minute
mir *(mir)* . . . . to me, me
mit *(mit)* . . . . with
Mittag, der *(mit-tahk)* . . . . noon
Mittagessen, das *(mit-tahk-ess-en)* . . . . lunch
Mitte, die *(mit-tuh)* . . . . middle
Mitternacht, die *(mit-tair-nahHt)* . . . . . . midnight
Mittwoch, der *(mit-vohH)* . . . . Wednesday
möchte *(murk-tuh)* . . . . (I, he, she, it) would like
möchten *(murk-ten)* . . . . . (we, they, you) would like
Moment, der *(moh-ment)* . . . . moment
Monat, der *(moh-naht)* . . . . month
Montag, der *(mohn-tahk)* . . . . Monday
morgen *(mor-gen)* . . . . tomorrow
Morgen, der *(mor-gen)* . . . . morning
morgens *(mor-gens)* . . . . . . mornings, in the morning
Moslem *(mohz-lem)* . . . . Moslem
Motorrad, das *(moh-tor-raht)* . . . . motorcycle
Mund, der *(moont)* . . . . mouth
Museum, das *(moo-zay-oom)* . . . . museum
Musik, die *(moo-zeek)* . . . . music
muß *(moos)* . . . . he, she, it must
müssen *(mew-sen)* . . . . to have to, must
Mutter, die *(moo-tair)* . . . . mother

N

nach *(nahH)* . . . . to, after
Nachmittag, der *(nahH-mit-tahk)* . . . . afternoon
nachmittags *(nahH-mit-tahgs)* . . . .
. . . . afternoons, in the afternoon
nächst *(nekst)* . . . . next
Nacht, die *(nahHt)* . . . . night
Nachthemd, das *(nahHt-hemt)* . . . . nightshirt
Nachtisch, der *(nahH-tish)* . . . . dessert
Name, der *(nah-muh)* . . . . name
Nation, die *(nah-tsee-ohn)* . . . . nation
Nationalität, die *(nah-tsee-oh-nahl-ih-tate)* . . nationality
natürlich *(nah-tewr-leeH)* . . . . naturally
neben *(nay-ben)* . . . . next to
neblig *(nay-blig)* . . . . foggy
nehmen *(nay-men)* . . . . to take
nein *(nine)* . . . . no
neu, neue, neuen *(noy)(noy-uh)(noy-en)* . . . . . . new
Neujahr, das *(noy-yar)* . . . . New Year's
neun *(noyn)* . . . . nine
neunzehn *(noyn-tsayn)* . . . . nineteen
neunzig *(noyn-tsig)* . . . . ninety
nicht *(neeHt)* . . . . no, not
nichts *(neeH-ts)* . . . . nothing
niedrig *(nee-drig)* . . . . low
noch *(nohH)* . . . . still, yet
Nord, der *(nort)* . . . . north
Nordamerika, das *(nort-ah-mair-ih-kah)* . . . .
. . . . North America
Nordpol, der *(nort-pohl)* . . . . North Pole
Nordsee, die *(nort-zay)* . . . . North Sea
Norwegen, das *(nor-vay-gen)* . . . . Norway
Notausgang, der *(noht-ows-gahng)* . . emergency exit
November, der *(noh-vem-bair)* . . . . November
null *(nool)* . . . . zero
Nummer, die *(noo-mair)* . . . . number
112 nun *(noon)* . . . . now

O

oben *(oh-ben)* . . . . above, upstairs
Obst, das *(ohpst)* . . . . fruit
Obstgeschäft, das *(ohpst-geh-sheft)* . . . . . . fruit store
oder *(oh-dair)* . . . . or
Ofen, der *(oh-fen)* . . . . oven
offen *(ohf-fen)* . . . . open
offiziell *(oh-fee-tsee-el)* . . . . official
Offizier, der *(oh-fih-tseer)* . . . . officer
öffnen *(uhf-nen)* . . . . to open
oft *(ohft)* . . . . often
ohne *(oh-nuh)* . . . . without
Ohr, das (or) . . . . ear
Ohrring, der *(or-ring)* . . . . earring
Oktober, der *(ohk-toh-bair)* . . . . October
Öl, das *(uhl)* . . . . oil
Omelett, das *(oh-meh-let)* . . . . omelette
Onkel, der *(ohn-kel)* . . . . uncle
Oper, die *(oh-pair)* . . . . opera
Opernhaus, das *(oh-pairn-house)* . . . . . . opera house
orange *(oh-rahn-zhuh)* . . . . orange (color)
Orangensaft, der *(oh-rahn-zhen-zahft)* . . orange juice
Orchester, das *(or-kes-tair)* . . . . orchestra
Ordnung, die *(ord-noong)* . . . . order
Organisation, die *(or-gahn-ih-zah-tsee-ohn)* . . . .
. . . . organization
Orgel, die *(or-gel)* . . . . organ
Österreich, das *(uh-stair-rike)* . . . . Austria
Ost, der *(ohst)* . . . . east
Ostern, das *(oh-stairn)* . . . . Easter
Ostküste, die *(ohst-kews-tuh)* . . . . east coast
Ozean, der *(oh-tsay-ahn)* . . . . ocean

P

packen *(pah-ken)* . . . . to pack
Paket, das *(pah-kate)* . . . . package
paniert *(pah-neart)* . . . . breaded
Papier, das *(pah-peer)* . . . . paper
Papierkorb, der *(pah-peer-korp)* . . wastepaper basket
Park, der *(park)* . . . . park
Parkplatz, der *(park-plahts)* . . . . parking space
parken *(par-ken)* . . . . to park
Paß, der *(pahs)* . . . . passport
Passagier, der *(pah-sah-zheer)* . . . . passenger
Paßkontrolle, die *(pahs-kohn-trohl-luh)* . . . .
. . . . passport control, check
passen *(pah-sen)* . . . . to fit
Pension, die *(pahn-see-ohn)* . . . . guest house
Personenzüge, die *(pair-zoh-nen-tsue-guh)* . local trains
Pfeffer, der *(fef-air)* . . . . pepper
Pfund, das *(foont)* . . . . pound
Photo, das *(foh-toh)* . . . . photograph
Physik, die *(fih-zeek)* . . . . physics
Pille, die *(pil-uh)* . . . . pill
Platz, der *(plahts)* . . . . space, place
Polen, das *(poh-len)* . . . . Poland
Police, die *(poh-lee-suh)* . . . . policy (insurance)
Politik, die *(poh-lih-teek)* . . . . politics
Polizei, die *(poh-lih-tsy)* . . . . police
Polnisch, das *(pohl-nish)* . . . . Polish (language)
Portugal, das *(por-too-gahl)* . . . . Portugal

Portugiesisch, das *(por-too-gee-zish)* . . . . Portuguese
Post, die *(post)* . . . . mail
Postamt, das *(post-ahmt)* . . . . post office
Postkarte, die *(pohst-kar-tuh)* . . . . postcard
Preis, der *(price)* . . . . price
Priester, der *(pree-stair)* . . . . priest
Problem, das *(pro-blame)* . . . . problem
Programm, das *(pro-grahm)* . . . . program
progressiv *(pro-gres-seev)* . . . . progressive
Pulli, der *(poo-lee)* . . . . sweater
purpur *(poor-poor)* . . . . purple

Q

Qualität, die *(kvah-lih-tate)* . . . . quality
Quantität, die *(kvahn-tih-tate)* . . . . quantity
Quittung, die *(kvih-toong)* . . . . receipt

R

radikal *(rah-dee-kahl)* . . . . radical
Radio, das *(rah-dee-oh)* . . . . radio
Rathaus, das *(raht-house)* . . . . city hall
Ratskeller, der *(rahts-kel-air)* . . . city-hall restaurant
Rasiermesser, das *(rah-zeer-mes-air)* . . . . razor
Rechnung, die *(rehH-noong)* . . . . bill
recht *(rehHt)* . . . . right, correct
rechts *(rehH-ts)* . . . . right
Regenmantel, der *(ray-gen-mahn-tel)* . . . . . raincoat
Regenschirm, der *(ray-gen-shirm)* . . . . . . umbrella
regnen *(rayg-nen)* . . . . to rain
reich *(rike)* . . . . rich
Reinigung, die *(ry-nih-goong)* . . . . cleaners
Reise, die *(ry-zuh)* . . . . trip, travel
Reisebüro, das *(ry-zuh-bew-roh)* . . . . travel office
reisen *(ry-zen)* . . . . to travel
Reisende, der *(ry-zen-duh)* . . . . traveler
Reiseschecks, die *(ry-zuh-shecks)* . . traveler's checks
Religion, die *(ray-lee-gee-ohn)* . . . . religion
Republik, die *(ray-poo-bleek)* . . . . republic
reservieren *(rez-air-veer-en)* . . . . to reserve
Reservierung, die *(rez-air-veer-oong)* . . reservation
Residenz, die *(ray-zih-dents)* . . . . residence
Restaurant, das *(res-toh-rahnt)* . . . . restaurant
Rettungsdienst, der *(ret-toongs-deenst)* . . rescue service
Richter, der *(reeH-tair)* . . . . judge
richtig *(reeH-teeg)* . . . . correct
Ring, der *(ring)* . . . . ring
Risiko, das *(ree-zee-koh)* . . . . risk
Ritter, der *(rit-tair)* . . . . knight
Rock, der *(rohk)* . . . . skirt
rosa *(roh-zah)* . . . . pink
Rose, die *(roh-zuh)* . . . . rose
rot *(roht)* . . . . red
Ruine, die *(roo-ee-nuh)* . . . . ruins
Rumänien, das *(roo-may-nee-en)* . . . . Romania
rund *(roont)* . . . . round
Russisch, das *(roo-sish)* . . . . Russian
Rußland, das *(roos-lahnt)* . . . . Russia

S

S-Bahn, die *(s-bahn)* . . . . streetcar
sagen *(zah-gen)* . . . . to say
Salat, der *(zah-laht)* . . . . salad
Salz, das *(zahlts)* . . . . salt

Samstag, der *(zahms-tahk)* . . . . Saturday
Sandalen, die *(zahn-dah-len)* . . . . sandals
sauber *(zow-bair)* . . . . clean
sauer *(zow-air)* . . . . sour
Schalter, der *(shahl-tair)* . . . . counter
scharf *(sharf)* . . . . sharp, spicy
Scheck, der *(sheck)* . . . . check
Schein, der *(shine)* . . . . bank note
Schiff, das *(shif)* . . . . ship
Schinken, der *(shink-en)* . . . . ham
Schlafanzug, der *(shlahf-ahn-tsook)* . . . . . pajamas
schlafen *(shlah-fen)* . . . . to sleep
Schlafwagen, der *(shlahf-vah-gen)* . . . . sleeping car
Schlafzimmer, das *(shlahf-tsih-mair)* . . . . bedroom
Schlagsahne, die *(shlahg-zah-nuh)* . . whipped cream
schlecht *(shlehHt)* . . . . bad
Schloß, das *(shlohs)* . . . . castle
schneien *(shny-en)* . . . . to snow
schnell *(shnel)* . . . . fast
Schnellimbiß, der *(shnel-im-biss)* . . refreshment bar
Schnellzüge, die *(shnel-tsue-guh)* . . . . . . fast trains
Schokolade, die *(shoh-koh-lah-duh)* . . . . . chocolate
schön *(shuhn)* . . . . pretty
Schottland, das *(shoht-lahnt)* . . . . Scotland
Schrank, der *(shrahnk)* . . . . closet, cupboard
schreiben *(shry-ben)* . . . . to write
Schreibtisch, der *(shripe-tish)* . . . . desk
Schreibwarenhandlung, die *(shripe-var-en-hahnt-loong)*
. . . . stationery store
Schuh, der *(shoo)* . . . . shoe
Schule, die *(shoo-luh)* . . . . school
schwarz *(shvarts)* . . . . black
Schweden, das *(shvay-den)* . . . . Sweden
Schwedisch, das *(shvay-dish)* . . . . Swedish
Schweiz, die *(shvites)* . . . . Switzerland
schwer *(shvair)* . . . . difficult, hard
Schwester, die *(shves-tair)* . . . . sister
schwimmen *(shvim-en)* . . . . to swim
sechs *(zeks)* . . . . six
sechzehn *(zeks-tsayn)* . . . . sixteen
sechzig *(zek-tsig)* . . . . sixty
See, die *(zay)* . . . . sea
sehen *(zay-en)* . . . . to see
sehr *(zair)* . . . . very
Seife, die *(zy-fuh)* . . . . soap
Seite, die *(zy-tuh)* . . . . page
Sekunde, die *(zay-koon-duh)* . . . . second
senden *(zen-den)* . . . . to send
September, der *(zep-tem-bair)* . . . . September
Serviette, die *(zair-vee-et-tuh)* . . . . napkin
Shorts, die *(shorts)* . . . . shorts
sie *(zee)* . . . . she, they
Sie *(zee)* . . . . you
sieben *(zee-ben)* . . . . seven
siebzehn *(zeep-tsayn)* . . . . seventeen
siebzig *(zeep-tsig)* . . . . seventy
Silvester, der *(sil-ves-tair)* . . . . New Year's Eve
sind *(zint)* . . . . they, we, you are
singen *(zing-en)* . . . . to sing
sitzen *(zit-tsen)* . . . . to sit
Ski, der *(she)* . . . . ski
Slowakei, die *(sloh-vah-ky)* . . . . Slovakia
so . . . wie *(zoh)* *(vee)* . . . . as . . . as
Socken, die *(zoh-ken)* . . . . socks

113

Sofa, das *(soh-fah)* . . . . sofa	**telefonieren** *(tay-lay-foh-neer-en)* . . . . to telephone
Sohn, der *(zohn)* . . . . son	**Telefonistin, die** *(tay-lay-foh-nee-stin)* . . . operator
Sommer, der *(zoh-mair)* . . . . summer	**Telefonkarte, die** *(tay-lay-fohn-kar-tuh)* . . . .
Sonne, die *(zoh-nuh)* . . . . sun	. . . . telephone card
Sonnenbrille, die *(zoh-nen-bril-luh)* . . . . . sunglasses	**Telefonzelle, die** *(tay-lay-fohn-tsel-luh)* . . . .
Sonntag, der *(zohn-tahk)* . . . . Sunday	. . . . telephone booth
Spanien, das *(shpah-nee-en)* . . . . Spain	**Telegramm, das** *(tay-lay-grahm)* . . . . telegram
Spanisch, das *(shpah-nish)* . . . . Spanish	**Teller, der** *(tel-air)* . . . . plate
spät *(shpay-t)* . . . . late	**Temperatur, die** *(tem-pair-ah-toor)* . . . temperature
Speise, die *(shpy-zuh)* . . . . food	**Tennisschuhe, die** *(ten-is-shoo-uh)* . . . . tennis shoes
Speisekarte, die *(shpy-zuh-kar-tuh)* . . . . . . menu	**Teppich, der** *(tep-eeH)* . . . . carpet
Speisewagen, der *(shpy-zuh-vah-gen)* . . . . dining car	**teuer** *(toy-air)* . . . . expensive
Spezialität, die *(shpay-tsee-ah-lih-tate)* . . . specialty	**Theaterkarte, die** *(tay-ah-tair-kar-tuh)* . . theater ticket
Spiegel, der *(shpee-gel)* . . . . mirror	**Thermometer, das** *(tair-moh-may-tair)* . . thermometer
Sport, der *(shport)* . . . . sport	**Tisch, der** *(tish)* . . . . table
sprechen *(shpreh-Hen)* . . . . to speak	**Tochter, die** *(tohH-tair)* . . . . daughter
Staat, der *(shtaht)* . . . . state, country	**Toilette, die** *(toy-let-tuh)* . . . . lavatory
Stadt, die *(shtaht)* . . . . city	**Tomatensaft, der** *(toh-mah-ten-zahft)* . . tomato juice
Stadtkarte, die *(shtaht-kar-tuh)* . . . . city map	**träumen** *(troy-men)* . . . . to dream
Stadtmitte, die *(shtaht-mit-tuh)* . . . . . city center	**trinken** *(trink-en)* . . . . to drink
Stiefel, die *(shtee-fel)* . . . . boots	**Trinkgeld, das** *(trink-gelt)* . . . . tip
Stock, das *(shtohk)* . . . . floor	**Tschechien, das** *(cheh-Hee-en)* . . . . . . Czech Republic
Straße, die *(shtrah-suh)* . . . . street	**Tschüs!** *(choos)* . . . . good-bye
Straßenbahn, die *(shtrah-sen-bahn)* . . . . . streetcar	**T-Shirt, das** *(tee-shirt)* . . . . t-shirt
Straßenbahnhaltestelle, die *(shtrah-sen-bahn-hahl-*	**Tuch, das** *(tooH)* . . . . towel
tuh-shtel-luh) . . . . streetcar stop	**tun** *(toon)* . . . . to do
Strumpfhose, die *(shtroomf-hoh-zuh)* . . . . panty hose	**Tür, die** *(tewr)* . . . . door
Stück, das *(shtewk)* . . . . piece	**typische** *(too-pish-uh)* . . . . typical
Student, der *(shtoo-dent)* . . . . student (male)	

U

Studentin, die *(shtoo-dent-in)* . . . . student (female)	**U-Bahn, die** *(oo-bahn)* . . . . subway
Stuhl, der *(shtool)* . . . . chair	**U-Bahnhaltestelle, die** *(oo-bahn-hahl-tuh-shtel-luh)*
Stunde, die *(shtoon-duh)* . . . . hour	. . . . subway stop
Sturm, der *(shturm)* . . . . storm	**U-Bahnkarte, die** *(oo-bahn-kar-tuh)* . . subway ticket
Süd *(zewt)* . . . . south	**über** *(ew-bair)* . . . . over, above
Südafrika, das *(zewt-ah-frih-kah)* . . . . South Africa	**Uhr, die** *(oor)* . . . . clock, watch
Südamerika, das *(zewt-ah-mair-ih-kah)*	**Uhrmacher, der** *(oor-mah-Hair)* . . . . . . watchmaker
. . . . South America	**um** *(oom)* . . . . around, at
Südpol, der *(zewt-pohl)* . . . . South Pole	**umsteigen** *(oom-shty-gen)* . . . . to transfer
Supermarkt, der *(zoo-pair-markt)* . . . . supermarket	**und** *(oont)* . . . . and
Suppe, die *(zoo-puh)* . . . . soup	**Ungarn, das** *(oon-garn)* . . . . Hungary
süß *(zoos)* . . . . sweet	**Ungarisch, das** *(oon-gar-ish)* . . . . Hungarian
Symphonie, die *(zoom-foh-nee)* . . . . symphony	**ungefähr** *(oon-geh-fair)* . . . . approximately
	uninteressant *(oon-in-tair-es-sahnt)* . . uninteresting

T

	Uniform, die *(oo-nee-form)* . . . . uniform
	Universität, die *(oo-nih-vair-zih-tate)* . . . . university
Tabakladen, der *(tah-bahk-lah-den)* . . . tobacco store	**unten** *(oon-ten)* . . . . below, downstairs
Tag, der *(tahk)* . . . . day	**unter** *(oon-tair)* . . . . under
Tagesgericht, das *(tah-ges-geh-reeHt)*	**Untergrund, der** *(oon-tair-groont)* . . . . subway
. . . . daily special	**Unterhemd, das** *(oon-tair-hemt)* . . . . . . undershirt
Tankstelle, die *(tahnk-shtel-luh)* . . . . . . gas station	**Unterhose, die** *(oon-tair-hoh-zuh)* . . . . . underpants
Tante, die *(tahn-tuh)* . . . . aunt	**Unterrock, der** *(oon-tair-rohk)* . . . . slip
Tanz, der *(tahn-ts)* . . . . dance	**unterwegs** *(oon-tair-vehgs)* . . . . in transit, on the way
tanzen *(tahn-tsen)* . . . . to dance	**Unterwelt, die** *(oon-tair-velt)* . . . . underworld

V

Taschentuch, das *(tah-shen-tooH)* . . . . handkerchief	
Tasse, die *(tah-suh)* . . . . cup	
tausend *(tau-zent)* . . . . thousand	**Vater, der** *(fah-tair)* . . . . father
Taxi, das *(tahk-see)* . . . . taxi	**Verb, das** *(vairb)* . . . . verb
Tee, der *(tay)* . . . . tea	**Verbindung, die** *(fair-bin-doong)* . . . . connection
Telefon, das *(tay-lay-fohn)* . . . . telephone	**verboten** *(fair-boh-ten)* . . . . prohibited
Telefonanruf, der *(tay-lay-fohn-ahn-roof)*	**Vereinigten Staaten, die** *(fair-eye-neeg-ten)(shtah-ten)*
. . . . telephone call	. . . . the United States
Telefonbuch, das *(tay-lay-fohn-booH)*	**verirren** *(fair-ear-en)* . . . . to go astray
. . . . telephone book	**verkaufen** *(fair-kow-fen)* . . . . to sell
Telefongespräch, das *(tay-lay-fohn-geh-shprayH)*	
. . . . telephone conversation	

verlieren *(fair-lear-en)* . . . . to lose
verstehen *(fair-shtay-en)* . . . . to understand
Verzeihung *(fair-tsy-oong)* . . . . excuse me
viel *(feel)* . . . . much, a lot
viel Glück *(feel)(glewk)* . . . . much luck,
viel Spaß *(feel)(shpahs)* . . . . much fun
vier *(fear)* . . . . four
Viertel, das *(fear-tel)* . . . . quarter
vierzehn *(fear-tsayn)* . . . . fourteen
vierzig *(fear-tsig)* . . . . forty
violett *(vee-oh-let)* . . . . violet
voll *(fohl)* . . . . full, drunk
Volk, das *(folk)* . . . . folk, people
vom *(=vom dem)* . . . . from the
vom Hammel *(fohm)(hah-mel)* . . . . . . mutton
vom Kalb *(fohm)(kahlp)* . . . . veal
vom Lamm *(fohm)(lahm)* . . . . lamb
vom Rind *(fohm)(rint)* . . . . beef
vom Schwein *(fohm)(shvine)* . . . . pork
von *(fohn)* . . . . from
vor *(for)* . . . . in front of
Vorfahrt, die *(for-fahrt)* . . . . right-of-way
Vorhang, der *(for-hahng)* . . . . curtain
Vorname, der *(for-nah-muh)* . . . . first name
Vorspeisen, die *(for-shpy-zen)* . . . . . . appetizers

W

Wagen, der *(vah-gen)* . . . . car
wandern *(vahn-dairn)* . . . . to wander
wann *(vahn)* . . . . when
war *(var)* . . . . was
Waren, die *(var-en)* . . . . wares
warm *(varm)* . . . . warm
Warnung, die *(var-noong)* . . . . warning
Wartesaal, der *(var-tuh-zahl)* . . . . . . waiting room
warum *(vah-room)* . . . . why
was *(vahs)* . . . . what
Waschbecken, das *(vahsh-beck-en)* . . . . . . sink
waschen *(vah-shen)* . . . . to wash
Wäscherei, die *(vesh-air-eye)* . . . . laundry
Wasser, das *(vah-sair)* . . . . water
Wechselstube, die *(veck-zel-shtoo-buh)* . . . .
. . . . money-exchange office
Wecker, der *(veck-air)* . . . . alarm clock
Weg, der *(veg)* . . . . way
Wein, der *(vine)* . . . . wine
Weihnachten, die *(vy-nahH-ten)* . . . . Christmas
Weihnachtsgeschenke, die *(vy-nahHts-geh-shen-kuh)*
. . . . Christmas presents
Weinglas, das *(wine-glahs)* . . . . wine glass
Weinstube, die *(vine-shtoo-buh)* . . . . . . wine cellar
weiß *(vice)* . . . . white
weiß *(vice)* . . . . he, she, it knows
Weißwein, der *(vice-vine)* . . . . white wine
weiter *(vy-tair)* . . . . further
welche, welches *(vel-chuh)(vel-ches)* . . . . which
wenig *(vay-nig)* . . . . few
wer *(vair)* . . . . who
Westküste, die *(vest-kews-tuh)* . . . . . . west coast
Westen, der *(ves-ten)* . . . . west
Westfälisch *(vest-fay-lish)* . . . . Westphalian (region)
Wetter, das *(vet-tair)* . . . . weather
wichtig *(veeH-teeg)* . . . . important
wie *(vee)* . . . . how

Wie geht es Ihnen? *(vee)(gate)(es)(ee-nen)* . . . .
. . . . How are you?
wieder *(vee-dair)* . . . . again
wiederholen *(vee-dair-hoh-len)* . . . . to repeat
wieviel *(vee-feel)* . . . . how much
Wild, das *(vilt)* . . . . venison, game
Willkommen, das *(vil-koh-men)* . . . . welcome
Wind, der *(vint)* . . . . wind
windig *(vin-dig)* . . . . windy
Winter, der *(vin-tair)* . . . . winter
wir *(vir)* . . . . we
wissen *(viss-en)* . . . . to know (a fact)
wo *(voh)* . . . . where
Woche, die *(voh-Huh)* . . . . week
wohl *(vohl)* . . . . well
wohnen *(voh-nen)* . . . . to live, reside
Wohnzimmer, das *(vohn-tsih-mair)* . . . . living room
Wolle, der *(voh-luh)* . . . . wool
Wort, das *(vort)* . . . . word
Wörter, die *(vur-tair)* . . . . words
Wörterbuch, das *(vur-tair-booH)* . . . . . . dictionary
wünschen *(vewn-shen)* . . . . to wish
Wurst, die *(vurst)* . . . . sausage

Z

Zahnbürste, die *(tsahn-bewr-stuh)* . . . . toothbrush
Zahnpaste, die *(tsahn-pah-stuh)* . . . . . . toothpaste
zehn *(tsayn)* . . . . ten
Zentimeter, der *(tsen-tih-may-tair)* . . . . . centimeter
zeigen *(tsy-gen)* . . . . to show
Zeitschrift, die *(tsight-shrift)* . . . . magazine
Zeitung, die *(tsy-toong)* . . . . newspaper
Zentimeter, der *(tsen-tih-may-tair)* . . . . centimeter
Zentrum, das *(tsen-troom)* . . . . center (of a city)
Zeremonie, die *(tsair-eh-moh-nee)* . . . . . ceremony
ziehen *(tsee-en)* . . . . to pull (doors)
Zigarre, die *(tsih-gah-ruh)* . . . . cigare
Zigarette, die *(tsih-gah-ret-tuh)* . . . . cigarette
Zimmer, das *(tsih-mair)* . . . . room
Zirkus, der *(tseer-koos)* . . . . circus
Zivilisation, die *(tsih-vih-lih-zah-tsee-ohn)* . . . .
. . . . civilization
Zoll, der *(tsohl)* . . . . customs
Zoo, der *(tsoh)* . . . . zoo
zu *(tsoo)* . . . . closed, to
Zucker, der *(tsoo-kair)* . . . . sugar
zu *(tsoo)* . . . . to, closed
Zug, der *(tsook)* . . . . train
Züge, die *(tsue-guh)* . . . . trains
zum *(= zu dem)* . . . . to the
zur *(= zu der)* . . . . to the
zusammen *(tsoo-zah-men)* . . . . together
zwanzig *(tsvahn-tsig)* . . . . twenty
zwei *(tsvy)* . . . . two
zweihundert *(tsvy-hoon-dairt)* . . . . . two hundred
zweiter *(tsvy-tair)* . . . . second
zwischen *(tsvih-shen)* . . . . between
zwölf *(ts-vulf)* . . . . twelve

Did you have fun learning your new language?
We at Bilingual Books hope you enjoy your
travels wherever they might take you!

This beverage guide is intended to explain the variety of beverages available to you while **in Deutschland oder** any other German-speaking country. It is by no means complete. Some of the experimenting has been left up to you, but this should get you started.

HEIßE GETRÄNKE (hot drinks)

Tasse Kaffee	cup of coffee
Kännchen Kaffee	pot of coffee
Glas Tee	cup of tea
Kännchen Tee	pot of tea
mit Zitrone	with lemon
mit Sahne	with cream

KALTE GETRÄNKE (cold drinks)

Spezi	½ cola, ½ Fanta
Apfelsaft	apple juice
Orangensaft	orange juice
Tomatensaft	tomato juice
Milch	milk
Orangenlimonade	orange drink
Zitronenlimonade	lemon-flavored drink
Mineralwasser	mineral water
mit Kohlensäure	carbonated
ohne Kohlensäure	non-carbonated
Apfelsaftschorle	apple juice and mineral water

SPIRITUOSEN (spirits)

Gin	gin
Rum	rum
Russischer Wodka	Russian vodka
Kirschwasser	cherry schnapps
Himbeergeist	raspberry schnapps
Williams-Birne	pear schnapps

APÊRITIFS (aperitifs)

Sherry	sherry
Portwein	port

BIERE (beers)

Bier is purchased in **Flaschen** (bottles) or **vom Faß** (draft).

Export vom Faß	draft export
Pils	pilsner
Diät-Pils	diet pilsner
Altbier	dark beer
Weizenbier	special wheat beer
Berliner Weiße	Berlin specialty —
(mit oder ohne	(with or without
Schuß-Waldmeister	a shot of Waldmeister
oder Himbeersirup)	or raspberry syrup)

WEINE (wines)

Wein is purchased by the **Flasche** (bottle) or **offen** (open, like a house wine).

Rotwein	red wine
Weißwein	white wine
Rosé	rosé
Tafelwein	table wine
Qualitätswein	quality wine
Kabinettwein	choice wine
Eiswein	ice wine (rare)
Schorle	wine mixed with mineral water

LIKÖRE (liqueurs)

Eierlikör	egg liqueur
Kirschlikör	cherry liqueur

GUT IM SOMMER

Erdbeerbowle	champagne, white wine, strawberries
Pfirsichbowle	champagne, white wine, peaches

GUT IM WINTER

Feuerzangenbowle	red wine, orange slices, spices, sugar block coated with rum, flambé

die Speisekarte
menu

Brot und Teigwaren (bread and pasta)

Brötchen	roll
Roggenbrot	rye bread
Schwarzbrot	brown bread
Weißbrot	white bread
Nudeln	noodles
Spätzle	type of noodle

Salate (salads)

Kopfsalat	lettuce
Bohnensalat	bean salad
Gemüsesalat	vegetable salad
Tomatensalat	tomato salad
Kartoffelsalat	potato salad
Endiviensalat	endive salad
Gurkensalat	cucumber salad
Selleriesalat	celery salad
Chicoreesalat	chicory salad
gemischter Salat	mixed salad
Geflügelsalat	chicken salad

Gemüse (vegetables)

Bohnen	beans
Erbsen	peas
Linsen	lentils
Spargel	asparagus
Karotten	carrots
Spinat	spinach
Lauch	leek
Tomaten	tomatoes
Pilze, Champignons	mushrooms
Weißkohl, Weißkraut	white cabbage
Rotkohl, Rotkraut	red cabbage
Blumenkohl	cauliflower
Rosenkohl	Brussels sprouts
rote Beete, rote Rübe	beets
Mais	corn
Gurken	cucumbers
Zwiebeln	onions
Radieschen	radish (small, red)
Rettich	radish (big, white root)
Meerrettich	horseradish
Kürbis	pumpkin

Kartoffeln (potatoes)

gekochte Kartoffeln,	
Salzkartoffeln	boiled potatoes
Bratkartoffeln,	
Röstkartoffeln	fried potatoes
Kartoffelgemüse	potatoes in cream sauce
Kartoffelpüree,	
Kartoffelbrei	mashed potatoes
Pommes Frites	French-fried potatoes
Kartoffelknödel	potato dumpling
Petersilienkartoffeln	parsley potatoes

Obst (fruit)

Apfel	apple
Apfelmus	applesauce
Birne	pear
Aprikose	apricot
Pfirsisch	peach
Banane	banana
Orange, Apfelsine	orange
Mandarine	tangerine
Kirsche	cherry
Pflaume, Zwetschge	plum
Mirabelle	sweet, yellow plum
Melone	melon
Pampelmuse, Grapefruit	grapefruit
Kompott	stewed fruit
Traube	grape

Beeren (berries)

Erdbeere	strawberry
Himbeere	respberry
Brombeere	blackberry
Stachelbeere	gooseberry
Johannisbeere	
(rot oder schwarz)	red or black currant
Preiselbeere	cranberry, red bilberry
Heidelbeere	blueberry

Art der Zubereitung (preparation)

im Backteig	in batter
gekocht	cooked, boiled
gebraten	roasted, fried
gebacken	baked
gedämpft	steamed
geschmort	braised
gegrillt	grilled
paniert	breaded
roh - englisch	rare
kurz angebraten	medium-rare
durchgebraten	well-done

Allgemeines (general)

Marmelade	jam
Gelee	jelly
Honig	honey
Salz	salt
Pfeffer	pepper
Öl	oil
Essig	vinegar
Senf	mustard
Soße	gravy
Aufschnitt	cold cuts
Käse	cheese
Nachtisch	dessert
Kuchen	cake
Gebäck	pastry, cookies
Eis	ice cream
Schlagsahne	whipped cream

(goo-ten) *(ah-peh-teet)*
Guten Appetit!
enjoy your meal

Vorspeisen (hors d'oeuvres)

Austern	oysters
Gänseleber-Pastete	goose-liver pâté
Heringsalat	herring salad
Kaviar	caviar
Raucheraal	smoked eel
Russische Eier	Russian eggs
Weinbergschnecken	snails
Hummer-Cocktail	lobster cocktail
Froschschenkel	frog's legs

Suppen (soups)

Kraftbrühe mit Ei	clear soup with egg
Tagessuppe	soup of the day
klare Fleischbrühe	beef broth
Hühnerbrühe	chicken broth
Bohnensuppe	bean soup
Erbsensuppe	pea soup
Linsensuppe	lentil soup
Kartoffelsuppe	potato soup
Champignoncremesuppe	cream-of-mushroom soup
Ochsenschwanzsuppe	oxtail soup
Gulaschsuppe	Hungarian goulash soup
Schildkrötensuppe	turtle soup
Königinsuppe	cream-of-chicken soup

Eierspeisen (eggs)

ein weich gekochtes Ei	one soft-boiled egg
ein hart gekochtes Ei	one hard-boiled egg
Spiegelei	fried egg
Rührei	scrambled eggs
verlorenes Ei	poached egg
Bauernomelett	farmer's omelette
Strammer Max	open ham sandwich, fried egg on top

Fleisch (meat)

vom Hammel, Hammelfleisch (mutton)

Hammelbraten	roast mutton
Hammelkotelett	mutton chop
Hammelkeule	leg of mutton
Lamm	lamb

vom Kalb, Kalbfleisch (veal)

Kalbsbraten	roast veal
Kalbsschnitzel	veal cutlet
Wiener Schnitzel	breaded veal cutlet
Paprika Schnitzel	red-pepper veal cutlet
Kalbsfrikassee	veal fricassee
Kalbshaxe	shank of veal
Kalbskeule	leg of veal
gefüllte Kalbsbrust	stuffed breast of veal
Kalbszunge	veal tongue
Kalbsleber	calf's liver
Kalbsrollbraten	rolled veal roast

vom Rind (beef)

Rindfleisch-	
Ochsenfleisch	broiled beef
Rindersaftbraten	braised beef
Ochsenbrust	boiled brisket of beef
Deutsches Beefsteak	Salisbury steak
Gulasch	Hungarian goulash
Schmorbraten	pot roast
Ochsenzunge	beef tongue
Filetgulasch Stroganoff	beef Stroganoff
Rinderroulade	stuffed, rolled beef slices
Wiener Rostbraten	cube steak with fried onions

vom Schwein, Schweinefleisch (pork)

Schweinebraten	roast pork
Schweineschnitzel	pork steak
Schweinekotelett	pork chop
Schweinelendchen	pork filet
Schweinshaxe	pig's knuckles (fried)
Schweineragout	ragout/stew
Hausmacher Bratwurst	homemade fried sausage
Eisbein	pig's knuckles (cooked)
Leberkäse	liver loaf
Schlachtplatte	hot pork sausages with sauerkraut

Geflügel (poultry)

Brathuhn	roast chicken
Hühnerfrikassee	chicken fricassee
Ente	duck
Gans	goose
Rebhuhn	partridge
Fasan	pheasant
Taube	pigeon
Truthahn/Puter	turkey

Wild (venison)

Hirschbraten	roast stag
Rehbraten	roast venison
Rehlendenbraten	filet roast of venison
Hirschkeule	leg of deer
Wildschweinbraten	roast wild boar
Wildschweinsteak	wild-boar steak
Hasenkeule	leg of hare
Hasenrücken	saddle of hare

Fisch (fish)

Schellfisch	haddock
Scholle (Flunder)	flounder
Heilbutt	halibut
Forelle	trout
Goldbarschfilet	bass filet
Kabeljau	cod
Seezunge	sole
Makrele	mackerel
Hecht	pike
Miesmuscheln	mussels
Krebse	crab
Karpfen	carp
Krabben	small shrimps
Ölsardinen	sardines (in oil)
Lachs/Raucherlachs	salmon/smoked salmon
Sardellen	anchovies
Aal	eel

FOLD HERE

(eeH)
ich

(vir)
wir

(air)
er

(zee)
Sie

(zee)
sie

(es,)
es

(koh-men)
kommen
(koh-muh)
ich komme

(gay-en)
gehen
(gay-uh)
ich gehe

(hah-ben)
haben
(hah-buh)
ich habe

(lair-nen)
lernen
(lair-nuh)
ich lerne

(brow-Hen)
brauchen
(brow-Huh)
ich brauche

(murk-ten)
möchten
(murk-tuh)
ich möchte

we	I
you	he
it	she or they
to go	to come
I go	I come
to learn	to have
I learn	I have
would like	to need
I would like	I need

(kow-fen)
kaufen
(kow-fuh)
ich kaufe

(beh-shtel-len)
bestellen
(beh-shtel-luh)
ich bestelle

(voh-nen)
wohnen
(voh-nuh)
ich wohne

(bly-ben)
bleiben
(bly-buh)
ich bleibe

(shpreh-Hen)
sprechen
(shpreh-Huh)
ich spreche

(hi-sen)
heißen
(hi-suh)
ich heiße

(ess-en)
essen
(ess-uh)
ich esse

(trink-en)
trinken
(trink-uh)
ich trinke

(zah-gen)
sagen
(zah-guh)
ich sage

(fair-shtay-en)
verstehen
(fair-shtay-uh)
ich verstehe

(fair-kow-fen)
verkaufen
(fair-kow-fuh)
ich verkaufe

(vee-dair-hoh-len)
wiederholen
(vee-dair-hoh-luh)
ich wiederhole

to order	to buy
I order	I buy
to remain/stay	to live/reside
I remain/stay	I live/reside
to be called	to speak
I am called/my name is	I speak
to drink	to eat
I drink	I eat
to understand	to say
I understand	I say
to repeat	to sell
I repeat	I sell

(fin-den)
finden

(fin-duh)
ich finde

(zay-en)
sehen

(zay-uh)
ich sehe

(zen-den)
senden

(zen-duh)
ich sende

(shlah-fen)
schlafen

(shlah-fuh)
ich schlafe

(mah-Hen)
machen

(mah-Huh)
ich mache

(beh-tsah-len)
bezahlen

(beh-tsah-luh)
ich bezahle

(tsy-gen)
zeigen

(tsy-guh)
ich zeige

(shry-ben)
schreiben

(shry-buh)
ich schreibe

(lay-zen)
lesen

(lay-zuh)
ich lese

(kuh-nen)
können

(kahn)
ich kann

(mew-sen)
müssen

(moos)
ich muß

(viss-en)
wissen

(vice)
ich weiß

to see	to find
I see	I find
to sleep	to send
I sleep	I send
to pay	to make/do
I pay	I make/do
to write	to show
I write	I show
to be able to/can	to read
I can	I read
to know (fact)	to have to/must
I know	I have to/must

(ahp-fah-ren)
abfahren

(tsook) *(fairt)* *(ahp)*
der Zug fährt ab

(flee-gen)
fliegen

(flee-guh)
ich fliege

(ry-zen)
reisen

(ry-zuh)
ich reise

(ahn-koh-men)
ankommen

(tsook) *(kohmt)* *(ahn)*
der Zug kommt an

(fah-ren)
fahren

(fah-ruh)
ich fahre

(oom-shty-gen)
umsteigen

(shty-guh) *(oom)*
ich steige um

(pah-ken)
packen

(pah-kuh)
ich packe

(zit-tsen)
sitzen

(zit-tsuh)
ich sitze

(gipt)
es gibt

(vah-shen)
waschen

(vah-shuh)
ich wasche

(gay-ben) *(zee)* *(mir)*
Geben Sie mir . . .

(fair-lear-en)
verlieren

(fair-lear-uh)
ich verliere

to fly	to depart
I fly	the train departs
to arrive	to travel
the train arrives	I travel
to transfer	to drive, travel by vehicle
I transfer	I drive
to sit	to pack
I sit	I pack
to wash	there is/there are
I wash	
to lose	give me . . .
I lose	

(hoy -tuh)
heute

(vee) *(gate)* *(es)* *(ee-nen)*
Wie geht es Ihnen?

(ges-tairn)
gestern

(bit-tuh)
bitte

(mor-gen)
morgen

(dahn-kuh)
danke

(owf) *(vee-dair-zay-en)*
Auf Wiedersehen!

(ent-shool-dee-goong)
Entschuldigung

(ahlt) *(noy)*
alt - neu

(vee-feel) *(koh-stet)* *(dahs)*
Wieviel kostet das?

(grohs) *(kline)*
groß - klein

(owf) *(tsoo)*
auf - zu

How are you?	today
please	yesterday
thank you	tomorrow
excuse me	good-bye
How much does this cost?	old - new
open - closed	large - small

gesund - krank
(geh-zoont) *(krahnk)*

gut - schlecht
(goot) *(shlehHt)*

heiß - kalt
(hice) *(kahlt)*

kurz - lang
(koorts) *(lahng)*

hoch - niedrig
(hohH) *(nee-drig)*

oben - unten
(oh-ben) *(oon-ten)*

links - rechts
(links) *(rehH-ts)*

langsam - schnell
(lahng-zahm) *(shnel)*

alt - jung
(ahlt) *(yoong)*

teuer - billig
(toy-air) *(bil-lig)*

arm - reich
(arm) *(rike)*

viel - wenig
(feel) *(vay-nig)*

good - bad

healthy - sick

short - long

hot - cold

above - below

high - low

slow - fast

left - right

expensive-
inexpensive

old - young

a lot - a little

poor - rich

Now that you've finished...

You've done it!

You've completed all the Steps, stuck your labels, flashed your cards and cut out your menu guide. Do you realize how far you've come and how much you've learned? You've accomplished what it could take years to achieve in a traditional language class.

You can now confidently

- ask questions,
- understand directions,
- make reservations,
- order food and
- shop anywhere.

And you can do it all in a foreign language! You can now go anywhere — from a large cosmopolitan restaurant to a small, out-of-the-way village where no one speaks English. Your experiences will be much more enjoyable and worry-free now that you speak the language and know something of the culture.

Yes, learning a foreign language can be fun. And no, not everyone abroad speaks English.

Kristine Kershul

* What about shipping costs?

STANDARD DELIVERY per address

If your items total	please add
up to $ 20.00	$5.00
$20.01 - $ 40.00	$6.00
$40.01 - $ 60.00	$7.00
$60.01 - $ 80.00	$8.00
$80.01 - $ 100.00	$9.00

If over $100, please call for charges.

For shipping outside the U.S., please call, fax or e-mail us at info@bbks.com for the best-possible shipping rates.

Bestellschein
order form

10 minutes a day® Series	QTY.	PRICE	TOTAL
CHINESE in 10 minutes a day®		$17.95	
FRENCH in 10 minutes a day®		$17.95	
GERMAN in 10 minutes a day®		$17.95	
HEBREW in 10 minutes a day®		$17.95	
INGLÉS en 10 minutos al día®		$17.95	
ITALIAN in 10 minutes a day®		$17.95	
JAPANESE in 10 minutes a day®		$17.95	
NORWEGIAN in 10 minutes a day®		$17.95	
PORTUGUESE in 10 minutes a day®		$17.95	
RUSSIAN in 10 minutes a day®		$19.95	
SPANISH in 10 minutes a day®		$17.95	

Language Map™ Series	QTY.	PRICE	TOTAL
CHINESE a language map™		$7.95	
FRENCH a language map™		$7.95	
GERMAN a language map™		$7.95	
GREEK a language map™		$7.95	
HAWAIIAN a language map™		$7.95	
HEBREW a language map™		$7.95	
INGLÉS un mapa del lenguaje™		$7.95	
ITALIAN a language map™		$7.95	
JAPANESE a language map™		$7.95	
NORWEGIAN a language map™		$7.95	
POLISH a language map™		$7.95	
PORTUGUESE a language map™		$7.95	
RUSSIAN a language map™		$7.95	
SPANISH a language map™		$7.95	
VIETNAMESE a language map™		$7.95	

† For delivery to individuals in Washington State, you must add 8.8% sales tax on the item total and the shipping costs combined. If your order is being delivered outside Washington State, you do not need to add sales tax.

Item Total	
* Shipping	+
Total	
† Sales Tax	+
ORDER TOTAL	

Name _____

Address _____

_____

City _____ State _____ Zip _____

Day Phone (_____) _____

❑ My check or money order for $_____ is enclosed.

Please make checks and money orders payable to Bilingual Books, Inc.

❑ Bill my credit card ❑ VISA ❑ MC ❑ AMEX

No. _____ Exp. date ____ / ____

Signature _____

Send us this order form with your check, money order or credit card details. If paying by credit card, you may fax your order to **(206) 284-3660** or call us toll-free at **(800) 488-5068**. All prices are in US dollars and are subject to change without notice.

Bilingual Books, Inc. • 1719 West Nickerson Street
Seattle, WA 98119 USA

Language Maps™
by Kristine K. Kershul

Finally a phrasebook which weighs only ounces, doesn't fall apart and can be dropped in a mud puddle without being ruined! A must for anyone traveling abroad!

A patented lamination process allows these handy *Language Maps*™ to fold and unfold in a snap without tearing. Each *Language Map*™ contains over 1,000 words and phrases split into important sections covering the basics for any trip.

A traveler's dream come true!

These attractive, flip-style *Language Maps*™ are also the perfect stocking stuffer, bon voyage gift, thank-you or party gift.

For languages available and information on how to order, please see our order form on the previous page. If you prefer, please call us at (206) 284-4211 or toll free at (800) 488-5068. You may also fax us at (206) 284-3660. E-mail: info@bbks.com.